Managing Editor
Mara Ellen Guckian

Editor in Chief
Karen J. Goldfluss, M.S. Ed.

Creative Director
Sarah M. Smith

Cover Artist
Barb Lorseyedi

Illustrator
Mark Mason

Art Coordinator
Renée Mc Elwee

Imaging
Craig Gunnell

Publisher
Mary D. Smith, M.S. Ed.

Author
Tracie Heskett, M.Ed.

Teacher Created Resources
12621 Western Avenue
Garden Grove, CA 92841
www.teachercreated.com

ISBN: 978-1-4206-3989-6

Reprinted, 2020
Made in U.S.A.

Table of Contents

Introduction

The *Healthy Habits for Healthy Kids* series was created to provide educators and parents with simple activities that help students learn to make healthy food choices, appreciate the importance of daily exercise, and develop healthy habits they will maintain throughout their lifetimes. Students who are healthy are better able to learn and be successful.

The activities in this book help students understand where the foods they eat come from and why nutritious food choices are beneficial to them. The objectives outlined by the USDA Food Guidance System *(ChooseMyPlate.gov)* formed the foundation upon which the activities in this book are based. Each of the five food groups is explored in depth. The goal is to build an understanding of the need to incorporate fruits, vegetables, whole grains, protein, and dairy into our daily diet. Students will also explore "sometimes" foods, or treats, and develop a greater understanding of why enjoying those foods in moderation is important to their health.

Physical fitness is also of the utmost importance for growing children, and it is suggested that they get at least 60 minutes per day of moderate to vigorous activity. At school and at home this can be difficult, because there is always so much to do. Still, knowing how important physical fitness is, we have to try! We have provided a variety of effective suggestions for exercises that can be done in the classroom. They can be completed in short increments on a daily basis. In addition to the obvious benefits of physical activity, the inclusion of purposeful physical activity at strategic times of the day can release tension and energize both students and teacher.

In recent years, the Common Core State Standards have been developed and are being implemented in many schools. These standards aim to prepare students for college and careers, with an emphasis on real-life applications. Coupled with the National Health Education Standards, they support a whole-child approach to education—one that ensures that each student is healthy, safe, engaged, supported, and challenged in his or her learning. The *Healthy Habits for Healthy Kids* series was developed to support this initiative.

How to Use This Book

The *Healthy Habits for Healthy Kids* series was developed to provide busy teachers and students with an easy-to-use curriculum to learn more about personal nutrition, health, and fitness. We want students to embrace making healthy food choices and getting exercise every day, knowing that healthier students make better learners.

Getting Started

- Share the Healthy Habits pledge (page 8) with students and discuss each line. Challenge students to learn the pledge and share it with family members. The goal here is to inspire the whole family to focus on good nutrition and support healthy habits.
- Post the pledge in the classroom and review it from time to time as students gain more insights into their personal health.
- Introduce daily exercise and breathing activities in class. On pages 11–12 you will find a list of simple movements and breathing exercises that students can do for a minute or two during the day. Display a clock with a second hand or keep a timer handy for these sessions. Use the physical activities to start the day and/or to transition from one activity to another. Throw in an extra one on tough days, or use more than one when weather conditions inhibit outdoor activity. These short, physical exercise breaks are a positive way to settle students for the day's work. And don't forget those breathing exercises! They can be done at any time of day and can help refocus or calm students as needed.

Introduction *(cont.)*

How to Use This Book *(cont.)*

Getting Started *(cont.)*

- Gather and display reference materials for the classroom on topics of nutrition, fitness, and overall health. Resources might include library or trade books, magazines, posters, and kid-friendly materials printed from government websites (see page 5). If appropriate, save links to relevant websites in a dedicated folder on classroom computers.
- Encourage students to start collecting packaging and nutritional labels from food products. Explain that they will be learning to read them and using them for comparisons. Establish an area in the classroom where these can be stored or displayed.

The Student Pages

Student pages present health-related information and activities. Discuss the information together as a class. Share information. Most activities require no more than writing implements and classroom research materials. Devote a certain amount of time each day or week to these activities. The more regular they are, the more important they will be for students.

You might consider interspersing the Healthy Foods activities with Healthy Habits activities to give students a balanced approach. As the teacher, you know how much information your students can absorb at a time. It is also important to be sensitive to the dietary needs and family eating habits of your students.

There are three sections to this book. The first section, Healthy Foods, focuses on the five food groups as described in government materials such as ChooseMyPlate.gov. The goal here is to educate students about healthy foods—what they look like, where they come from, what nutrients they provide, and how they can be incorporated into one's diet. A list of the foods in the food group is found at the beginning of each section. Have students think about the foods they eat regularly, the foods they have not heard of before, and healthy foods they would like to try. Provide resource materials for students to learn about foods that are new to them. Encourage students to think about ways they can make healthy food choices each day. Students will also learn about nutrition, including calories, carbohydrates, protein, and vitamins and minerals and the roles these nutrients play in overall health.

In the Healthy Habits section, students are introduced to concepts such as food safety, germ prevention, dental care, physical fitness, and other ways to stay safe and healthy.

Fruits
Grains
Dairy
Vegetables
Protein
ChooseMyPlate.gov

Suggestions on pages 80–81 are for outdoor and gross-motor skills activities. These activities will allow students to explore a full range of motion: hopping, skipping, running, leaping, jumping, etc.

The final section of this book is devoted to journaling. The student journal gives students the opportunity to express their thoughts about the information presented in the activities and class discussions. It can be used for reflective writing, sorting or summarizing information, or to check for understanding.

Reproduce copies of the journal pages for each student. You may wish to have students add pages to the journal throughout the year as new food and fitness topics arise. Students can add notebook paper to the journal, or you can reproduce extra copies of the blank journal page that is provided on page 92.

The CD includes ready-to-print PDF files of the student activity pages and the "Food and Fitness Journal," as well as correlations to the Common Core State Standards and the National Health Education Standards.

Internet Resources

These sites provide useful, age-appropriate information to aid you in embarking on a year filled with active, healthy students. Let's move!

Action for Healthy Kids
This site provides information for schools, students, and parents, as well as programs to promote active, healthy lifestyles for kids.
http://www.actionforhealthykids.org/

CDC BAM! Body and Mind
This site was designed for 9–13-year-olds. BAM! provides information kids need to make healthy lifestyle choices.
http://www.cdc.gov/bam/teachers/index.html

Fresh for Kids
This site offers resources for kids and teachers, including informative pages on specific fruits and vegetables.
http://www.freshforkids.com.au

Let's Move! America's Move to Raise a Healthier Generation of Kids
This program was developed by First Lady Michelle Obama to solve the epidemic of childhood obesity.
http://www.letsmove.gov

National Farm to School Network
This site offers resources and information about farm-to-school programs in each state.
http://www.farmtoschool.org

Nourish Interactive
This site offers free printable activities based on the *ChooseMyPlate.gov* food groups.
http://www.nourishinteractive.com/nutrition-education

Tips for Healthy Eating–Ten Healthy Habits for Kids
This site includes a summary of ways families can incorporate healthy eating habits.
http://www.nestle.com/nhw/health-wellness-tips/healthy-habits-kids

USDA—United States Department of Agriculture
This site includes kid-friendly research, printable materials, and Nutrition Fact Cards.
http://www.choosemyplate.gov/print-materials-ordering.html

The Whole Child
This site focuses on ensuring that each child, in each school, in each community is healthy, safe, engaged, supported, and challenged to meet the demands of the 21st century.
http://www.wholechildeducation.org

Whole Grains Council
The Whole Grains Council wants to support everyone who's helping spread the word about the health benefits of whole grains, and about easy ways to find and enjoy more whole grains.
http://wholegrainscouncil.org/resources/educational-materials

National Health Education Standards

The activities in *Healthy Habits for Healthy Kids* (*Grades 3 and 4*) meet the following National Health Education Standards. For more information about these standards go to *www.cdc.gov/healthyyouth/sher/standards/index.htm*

Standard 1. Students will comprehend concepts related to health promotion and disease prevention to enhance health.
Standard 1.5.1 Describe the relationship between healthy behaviors and personal health.
Standard 1.5.2 Identify examples of emotional, intellectual, physical, and social health.
Standard 1.5.3 Describe ways in which safe and healthy school and community environments can promote personal health.
Standard 1.5.4 Describe ways to prevent common childhood injuries and health problems.
Standard 1.5.5 Describe when it is important to seek health care.
Standard 2. Students will analyze the influence of family, peers, culture, media, technology, and other factors on health behaviors.
Standard 2.5.1 Describe how the family influences personal health practices and behaviors.
Standard 2.5.2 Identify the influence of culture on health practices and behaviors.
Standard 2.5.3 Identify how peers can influence healthy and unhealthy behaviors.
Standard 2.5.4 Describe how the school and community can support personal health practices and behaviors.
Standard 2.5.5 Explain how media influences thoughts, feelings, and health behaviors.
Standard 2.5.6 Describe ways that technology can influence personal health.
Standard 3. Students will demonstrate the ability to access valid information, products, and services to enhance health.
Standard 3.5.1 Identify characteristics of valid health information, products, and services.
Standard 3.5.2 Locate resources from home, school, and community that provide valid health information.
Standard 4. Students will demonstrate the ability to use interpersonal communication skills to enhance health and avoid or reduce health risks.
Standard 4.5.1 Demonstrate effective verbal and nonverbal communication skills to enhance health.
Standard 4.5.2 Demonstrate refusal skills that avoid or reduce health risks.
Standard 4.5.3 Demonstrate nonviolent strategies to manage or resolve conflict.
Standard 4.5.4 Demonstrate how to ask for assistance to enhance personal health.
Standard 5. Students will demonstrate the ability to use decision-making skills to enhance health.
Standard 5.5.1 Identify health-related situations that might require a thoughtful decision.
Standard 5.5.2 Analyze when assistance is needed in making a health-related decision.
Standard 5.5.3 List healthy options to health-related issues or problems.
Standard 5.5.4 Predict the potential outcomes of each option when making a health-related decision.
Standard 5.5.5 Choose a healthy option when making a decision.
Standard 5.5.6 Describe the outcomes of a health-related decision.
Standard 6. Students will demonstrate the ability to use goal-setting skills to enhance health.
Standard 6.5.1 Set a personal health goal and track progress toward its achievement.
Standard 6.5.2 Identify resources to assist in achieving a personal health goal.
Standard 7. Students will demonstrate the ability to practice health-enhancing behaviors and avoid or reduce health risks.
Standard 7.5.1 Identify responsible personal health behaviors.
Standard 7.5.2 Demonstrate a variety of healthy practices and behaviors to maintain or improve personal health.
Standard 7.5.3 Demonstrate a variety of behaviors to avoid or reduce health risks.
Standard 8. Students will demonstrate the ability to advocate for personal, family, and community health.
Standard 8.5.1 Express opinions and give accurate information about health issues.
Standard 8.5.2 Encourage others to make positive health choices.

Common Core State Standards Correlation

The lessons and activities included in *Healthy Habits for Healthy Kids (Grades 3 and 4)* meet the following Common Core State Standards. (©Copyright 2010. National Governors Association Center for Best Practices and Council of Chief State School Officers. All rights reserved.) For more information about these standards, go to *http://www.corestandards.org/* or visit *http://www.teachercreated.com/standards/* for activites related to each standard.

Reading: Informational Text
Key Ideas and Details
ELA.RI.3.1 Ask and answer questions to demonstrate understanding of a text, referring explicitly to the text as the basis for the answers.
ELA.RI.4.1 Refer to details and examples in a text when explaining what the text says explicitly and when drawing inferences from the text.
Craft and Structure
ELA.RI.3.4 Determine the meaning of general academic and domain-specific words and phrases in a text relevant to a *grade 3 topic or subject area.*
ELA.RI.4.4 Determine the meaning of general academic and domain-specific words or phrases in a text relevant to a *grade 4 topic or subject area.*
ELA.RI.3.5 Use text features and search tools to locate information relevant to a given topic efficiently.
Integration of Knowledge and Ideas
ELA.RI.4.7 Interpret information presented visually, orally, or quantitatively and explain how the information contributes to an understanding of the text in which it appears.
Writing
Text Types and Purposes
ELA.W.3.1 Write opinion pieces on topics or texts, supporting a point of view with reasons.
ELA.W.4.1 Write opinion pieces on topics or texts, supporting a point of view with reasons and information.
ELA.W.3.2 Write informative/explanatory texts to examine a topic and convey ideas and information clearly.
ELA.W.4.2 Write informative/explanatory texts to examine a topic and convey ideas and information clearly.
Research to Build and Present Knowledge
ELA.W.3.7 Conduct short research projects that build knowledge about a topic.
ELA.W.4.7 Conduct short research projects that build knowledge through investigation of different aspects of a topic.
Range of Writing
ELA.W. 3.10 Write routinely over extended time frames and shorter time frames for a range of discipline-specific tasks, purposes, and audiences.
ELA.W. 4.10 Write routinely over extended time frames and shorter time frames for a range of discipline-specific tasks, purposes, and audiences.
Speaking and Listening
Comprehension and Collaboration
ELA .SL.3.1 Engage effectively in a range of collaborative discussions with diverse partners on *grade 3 topics and texts,* building on others' ideas and expressing their own clearly.
ELA .SL.4.1 Engage effectively in a range of collaborative discussions with diverse partners on *grade 4 topics and texts,* building on others' ideas and expressing their own clearly.
Language
Conventions of Standard English
ELA.L.3.1 Demonstrate command of the conventions of standard English grammar and usage when writing or speaking.
ELA.L.4.1 Demonstrate command of the conventions of standard English grammar and usage when writing or speaking.
Vocabulary Acquisition and Use
ELA.L.3.4 Determine or clarify the meaning of unknown and multiple-meaning words and phrases based on *grade 3 reading and content,* choosing flexibly from a range of strategies.
ELA.L.4.4 Determine or clarify the meaning of unknown and multiple-meaning words and phrases based on *grade 4 reading and content,* choosing flexibly from a range of strategies.

Take the Pledge

Directions: Read and practice the "Healthy Habits Pledge." When you are ready, recite it to a friend or family member. Sign your name at the bottom of the pledge when you have completed this activity and bring the page back to school.

Healthy Habits Pledge

I pledge to stay healthy and clean
through exercise and good hygiene.
I will eat balanced meals every day
to have more energy to learn and to play.
Every night I will get a good rest
to be more ready to do my best.
If I work hard to be healthy and strong
I'll be happier my whole life long.

I, ______________________________, have read and learned the Healthy Habits Pledge.

Directions: Write at least one personal health goal you would like to meet this week. Check in a week and see how you're doing at meeting your goal. Read the pledge again and continue adding goals using your "Personal Health Goal" journal page.

______________________________'s Personal Goal	Met	Not Yet
Week ____________________ My personal goal this week is to ____________________ ______________________________ ______________________________ ______________________________ ______________________________		

Introducing the 5 Food Groups

Fruits

apples	grape juice	mangoes	plums
apple juice	grapefruit	nectarines	raisins
apricots	grapefruit juice	orange juice	raspberries
bananas	grapes	oranges	starfruit
blackberries	honeydew	papayas	strawberries
blueberries	kiwi fruit	peaches	tangerines
cantaloupe	lemons	pears	watermelon
cherries	limes	pineapples	

Culinary or Fruit Vegetables

avocado	green beans	pumpkin	red peppers
cucumber	green peppers	squash	tomatoes

Vegetables

artichoke	cauliflower	kidney beans	romaine lettuce
asparagus	celery	leaf lettuce	soybeans
bean sprouts	collard greens	lentils	spinach
beets	corn	lima beans	split peas
black beans	dry black-eyed peas	mushrooms	sweet potatoes
bok choy	eggplant	navy beans	taro
broccoli	garbanzo beans	onions	turnips
Brussels sprouts	(chickpeas)	peas	watercress
cabbage	iceberg lettuce	pinto beans	wax beans
carrots	kale	potatoes	white beans

Important Distinctions

We define *fruit* as the sweet, fleshy part of a plant. Any part of a plant we eat that is *not* the fruit might be considered a vegetable. By this definition, vegetables can include *leaves, stems, roots, flowers, bulbs,* and *seeds.*

Culinary or Fruit Vegetables—We know that *fruit* refers to the flowering part of a plant in which seeds develop. By this definition, many foods we consider vegetables are actually fruits. Often, these foods are prepared or eaten as vegetables, so we call them "culinary vegetables" or "fruit vegetables."

Teacher Note: This book refers to the five food groups as listed on ChooseMyPlate.gov *http://www.choosemyplate.gov*. The tables on pages 9 and 10 list foods in their true columns. See the notes above for exceptions for purposes of discussion with students.

Introducing the 5 Food Groups *(cont.)*

Grains

Whole Grains		Refined Grains Foods
amaranth	rye	cereals
barley	sorghum	corn tortillas
brown rice	triticale	cornbread
buckwheat	whole grain cereal	couscous
bulger (cracked wheat)	whole wheat bread	crackers
cornmeal	whole wheat crackers	flour tortillas
millet	whole wheat pasta	grits
muesli	whole wheat rolls	noodles
oatmeal	whole wheat tortillas	pasta
popcorn	wild rice	pitas
quinoa		white bread
rolled oats		white rice

Dairy

- cheddar cheese
- cottage cheese
- frozen yogurt
- Greek yogurt
- milk
- mozzarella cheese
- parmesan cheese
- pudding
- ricotta cheese
- swiss cheese
- yogurt

Protein

- almonds
- beef
- bison
- black beans
- black-eyed peas
- cashews
- chicken
- chickpeas (garbanzo beans)
- duck
- eggs
- fish
- goose
- ham
- hazelnuts
- kidney beans
- lamb
- lima beans
- navy beans
- nuts
- peanuts
- pecans
- pinto beans
- pistachios
- pork
- pumpkin seeds
- rabbit
- sesame seeds
- shellfish
- soybeans
- split peas
- sunflower seeds
- tuna
- turkey
- veal
- venison
- walnuts

* *also* ground meat including beef, chicken, lamb, pork, and turkey

Name

Exercise of the Day

Here are some exercises you can do to start the day or during a "movement break" in the classroom. Challenge yourself to do a few more repetitions each time you do the exercise. Remember though, it is more important to do them correctly to protect your muscles and joints than it is to do them fast!

- ☐ Pretend to hula-hoop for 30 seconds. Move your hips!
- ☐ Hop on one foot 10 times then on the other foot 10 times.
- ☐ Run in place for 1 minute.
- ☐ Do 30 jumping jacks.
- ☐ Hold your arms out shoulder height. Make 10 small circles with your arms. Reverse directions and do 10 more. Then make 10 large circles with your arms. Reverse directions and do 10 more.
- ☐ Do windmills. Bend at the waist and touch your left hand to your right foot and then switch sides. How many windmills (one left, one right) can you do in 1 minute?
- ☐ March in place for 1 minute. Swing your arms forward and back and lift your knees waist high (if you can).
- ☐ Pretend to climb stairs for 1 minute.
- ☐ Stand with your feet about 6 inches apart. "Sit back" and do 15 squats. Try not to have your knees go past your toes.
- ☐ Do 10 lunges on each leg. Your knee should be above your ankle, and not any farther.
- ☐ Do as many pushups with your hands on your desk as you can. The next time, try to improve your score.
- ☐ How many crunches can you do in 30 seconds? Remember, you have to have your elbows touch your knees each time.
- ☐ Do chair squats. Stand up just before you sit in your chair.
- ☐ Sit on your chair and move your legs as if you are riding a bicycle.
- ☐ Do calf raises. Stand on your tiptoes and reach your hands straight out or straight up.
- ☐ Do standing standing leg raises. Place your hands on the back of a chair, bend your knee, and raise your leg perpendicular to floor.
- ☐ Do wall pushups for 30 seconds.
- ☐ Do 10 wall squats, with your back flat against the wall.
- ☐ Do 10 leg raises for each leg. Sit on your chair, raise one leg, then straighten it, and then put it back down.
- ☐ Raise both legs at the same time while seated. How many times can you do this in one minute?

Name

Exercise of the Day *(cont.)*

Explain to students that deep breathing, bending, stretching, and balance exercises help us to relax and to focus. Relaxing helps take away stress. When we return to our schoolwork after a bit of physical activity or a deep breathing exercise we can think more clearly.

As a group, agree that each person will focus on his or her own movements. No one will tease or bother anyone else.

Breathing Activities

Steady breathing can help you calm down and relax. See which of these techniques works best for you.

- ☐ Close your eyes and pull air as deep into your lungs as you can. Feel them expand. Breathe out as much air as you can. Keep each breath steady.
- ☐ Breathe in for the count of four. Hold the breath for the count of four. Breathe out for the count of four. Try not to take another breath for the count of four. Then try breathing in and out for 5, then 6, etc.
- ☐ Breathe in through your nose. Breathe out through your mouth, quietly saying "haaa." Focus on the breathing "out." Your body will do the breathing "in" for you.

Balancing Exercises

- ☐ Balance on one foot for 30 seconds. Hold the other leg up with a bent knee. Then balance on the other foot. Try this exercise with your eyes closed.
- ☐ Walk on a straight line (tape or a line on the floor) for 20 paces. Try it with your hands stretched out from your sides, then try it with your hands straight down next to your sides. Which is easier?

Stretching Exercises

We are not all flexible in the same way. Treat your body with respect and don't try to do what your neighbor is doing. Do a stretch that feels good for your own body. With practice, you may stretch farther, but you may not. It depends on how flexible your body can be. That is why it is important to respect your own body and not be competitive. The goal of these exercises is to help you relax and be able to focus on your work.

- ☐ Sit and bend from your waist to the right, then to the left. Do this 15 times on each side.
- ☐ Stand with your legs apart. Bend over from your waist, bending your knees a little. Let your arms hang down. Sway gently side-to-side.
- ☐ Sit on the floor and put the soles of your feet together. Sit up straight as tall as you can. Imagine there is a string attached to your head (like a puppet) gently pulling you up.
- ☐ Lie on your belly. Breathe in. Relax as you breathe out. Bend your knees and hold your ankles behind you. Breathe in and gently lift your head, chest, and legs off the floor. Lift your head and feet toward the ceiling to stretch. Breathe out as you come back down to the floor. Some people will be able to stretch up a lot and others not as far.

Steps to Healthy Eating

1. Choose servings the size of your fist.

2. Have fruits and vegetables on half of your plate. Can you do it for all three meals?

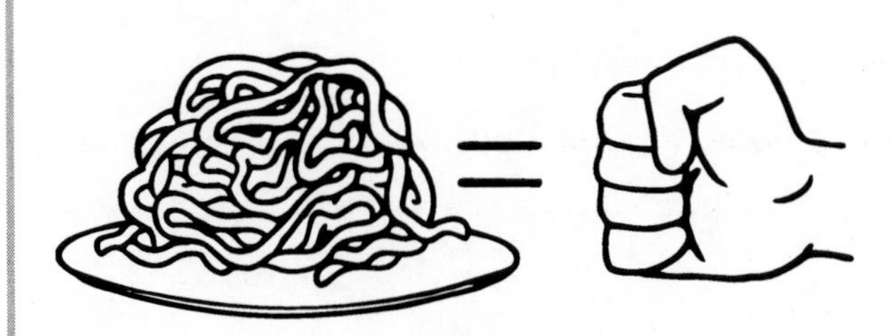

3. Enjoy water as your favorite drink. Make it a habit!

4. Eat foods from each food group for a balanced diet.

5. Choose foods with less sugar and fat to avoid "empty" calories.

Name

Food Groups

One way to stay healthy and strong is to eat foods that are good for us. Healthy foods have important nutrients we need for our growth and development to keep our bodies healthy in many ways.

We make choices about the food we eat each day. One way to make healthy choices is to eat different kinds of food. We divide the food we eat into 5 groups—*Fruits, Vegetables, Grains, Dairy,* and *Protein.* It is best if we eat foods from each food group every day. Eating a variety of foods will help us get all the different nutrients we need.

Directions: What foods do you think might belong in each food group? Write or draw your ideas on the plate.

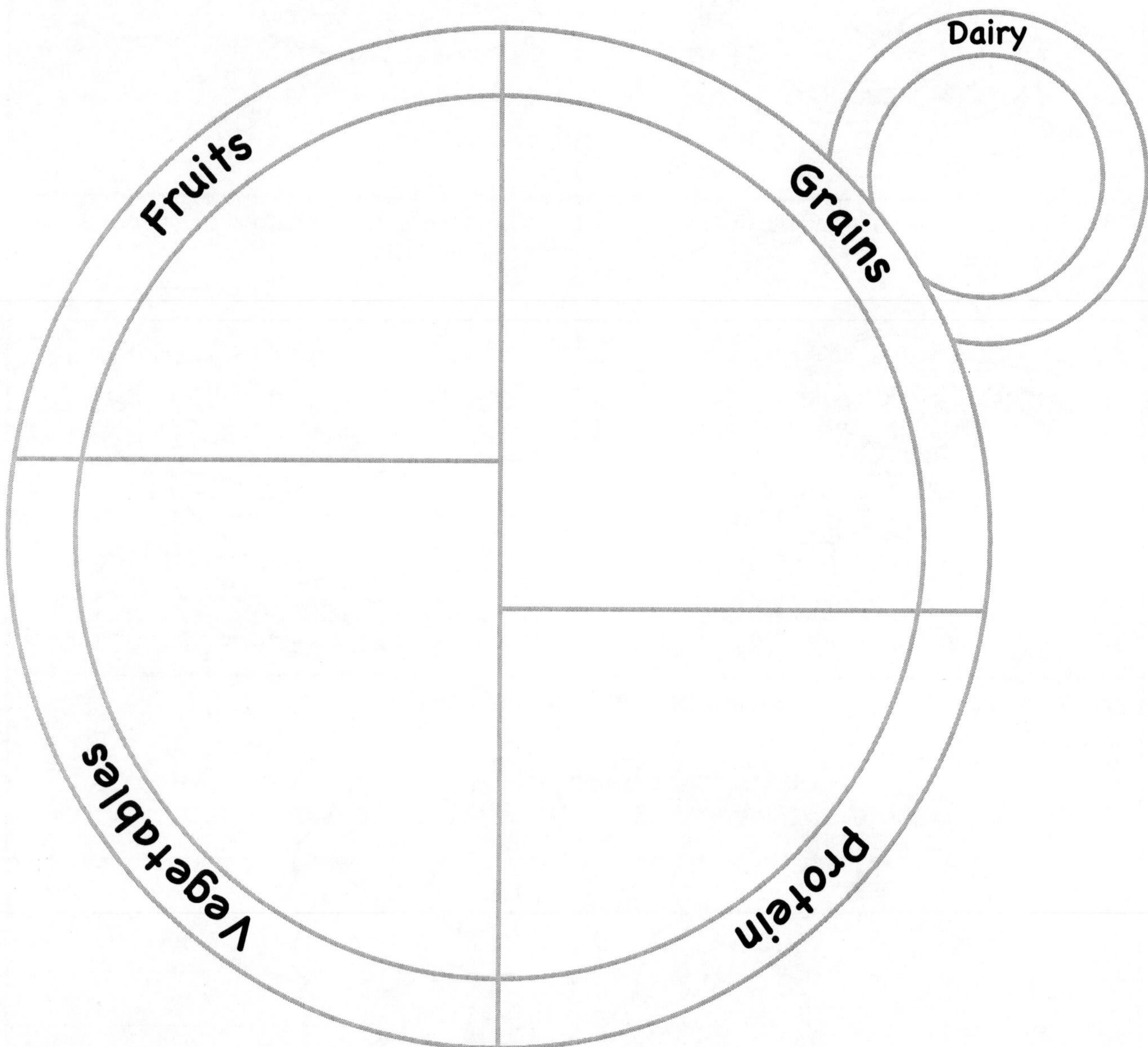

Teacher Note: The outline above is based on the USDA MyPlate graphic. See page 5 for information and the website.

Name

My Plate

Directions: Think about the foods you ate yesterday for breakfast, lunch, snacks, and dinner. Write them in the correct spaces on the chart. Add foods that don't fit in the five food groups in the section titled "Other" at the bottom.

The Five Food Groups				
Protein	**Dairy**	**Vegetables**	**Fruits**	**Grains**
Other				

1. Which food groups might you need to eat more of? ____________________

   Why? ____________________

2. How might you change what you eat to have a more balanced diet? ____________________

   ____

   ____

Name

Think About Fruit

Fruit is one of the healthy food groups. We define *fruit* as the sweet, fleshy part of a plant that has the seed or seeds of the plant. Eating fruit helps keep your heart healthy. A healthy heart pumps blood through the body effectively. Healthy foods, like fruits, also lower the risk of disease, such as cancer and diabetes. Fruit has many vitamins and other nutrients, including the following:

Vitamin C—Vitamin C helps our bodies heal if we get a cut. It helps tissues inside our bodies heal, too. It helps us have strong bones and teeth.

Potassium—Potassium helps our nerves and muscles function the way they should. It helps our hearts beat properly.

Fiber—Fiber helps us digest our food so our bodies can use it for energy.

Folic Acid—Folic acid is a type of B vitamin. It helps our bodies make red blood cells. Red blood cells carry oxygen from our lungs to all parts of our body.

Vitamin C
Potassium
Fiber
Protein

Directions: Did you know there were so many different fruits? Check the boxes of the fruits you have eaten. Put an **X** in boxes next to fruits you have not tried yet. Circle your three favorite fruits.

Fruits

- ☐ apples
- ☐ apricots
- ☐ bananas
- ☐ blackberries
- ☐ blueberries
- ☐ boysenberries
- ☐ cantaloupe
- ☐ cherries
- ☐ Crenshaw melon
- ☐ coconut
- ☐ cranberries
- ☐ dragon fruit
- ☐ figs
- ☐ grapefruit
- ☐ grapes
- ☐ guavas
- ☐ honeydew
- ☐ kiwi fruit
- ☐ kumquat
- ☐ lemons
- ☐ limes
- ☐ mangoes
- ☐ nectarines
- ☐ oranges
- ☐ papayas
- ☐ passion fruit
- ☐ peaches
- ☐ pears
- ☐ persimmon
- ☐ pineapples
- ☐ plums
- ☐ pomegranates
- ☐ raisins
- ☐ raspberries
- ☐ star fruit
- ☐ strawberries
- ☐ tangerines
- ☐ watermelon

Name

Think About Fruit *(cont.)*

Directions:

1. Use the list of fruits on page 16. Research two fruits that are new to you.
2. Fill in the information about each fruit and draw a picture of it.

Fruit: ______	**Fruit:** ______
Color: ______	**Color:** ______
Shape: ______	**Shape:** ______
Size: ______	**Size:** ______
It comes from ______	**It comes from** ______
It is good for me because it has ______.	**It is good for me because it has** ______.

Directions: Use page 16 to help answer the following questions.

1. Bananas are a good source of potassium. Potassium helps my ______ and ______ work well.
2. Apples, berries, and figs are good sources of fiber. Fiber helps digest foods to give me ______.
3. Oranges and grapefruit are a good source of folic acid, which makes red ______ ______.
4. Red blood cells carry oxygen from our ______ to all parts of our body.

Name

How Does Fruit Grow?

Most of us buy fruit from a store, but where does fruit come from? How does it grow?

- Some fruits, like oranges and apples, grow on trees. Many fruit trees need cross-pollination. This means they need to have pollen carried from one variety of tree to another tree to produce fruit. For example, a Red Delicious apple tree can be pollinated by a Jonathan apple tree. Insects, birds, and the wind can carry pollen from one tree to another.
- Fruits like blueberries grow on bushes. Blueberries will produce more fruit if they have other plants for pollen. Strawberries grow on bushes very low to the ground.
- Raspberries grow on thorny brambles, also known as canes.

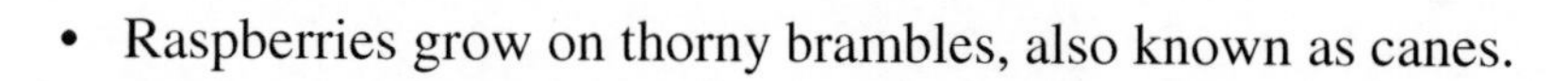

- Grapes grow on vines. Most vine fruits need a warm climate with a long growing season. This fruit takes patience to grow because it ripens best on the vine. Most vine fruits, except kiwi fruit, do not need other plants for pollen.

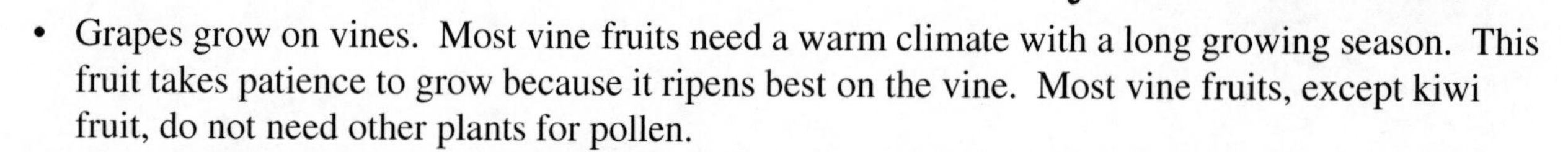

Directions: Work with a partner to brainstorm a list of different fruits. Write each fruit in the correct column to show how it grows. If you don't know, do some research. Discuss which kinds of fruits grow in your area. Add them to the list and put a star next to them.

Tree Fruits	Bush Fruits	Bramble Fruits	Vine Fruits

Challenge: We call peppers vegetables, but they are actually fruits. They have seeds on the inside.

1. How many "fruit vegetables" like peppers can you think of that grow on vines?

____

____

2. Research to learn more about fruits that grow on vines that we eat as vegetables. What did you learn?

____

____

Name

Fruit Seeds We Eat

Pomegranates have been around a long time. It takes just the right amount of sun and water to grow pomegranate fruit. Pomegranates grow on large bushes or small trees. The fruit is about the size of a medium orange. The fruit has red-pink skin that is like leather.

People eat the seeds of the pomegranate. The small seeds provide fiber. Pomegranate juice is very good for you, too. Pomegranate juice has vitamins C and E, potassium, and iron.

How do you get seeds out of a pomegranate? That can be tricky! Try this with an adult:

1. Cut the top off the pomegranate.

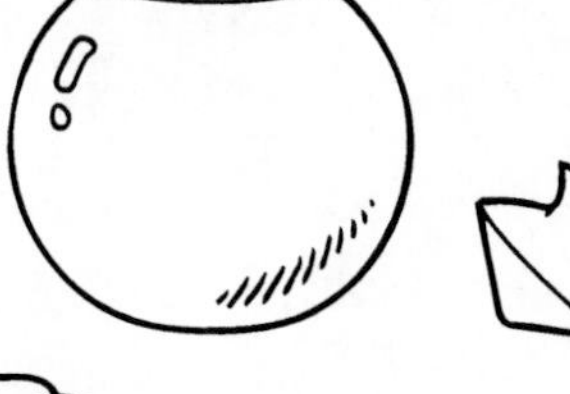

2. Slice it into sections.

3. Break the sections into pieces. Pull the skin (membrane) off each section.

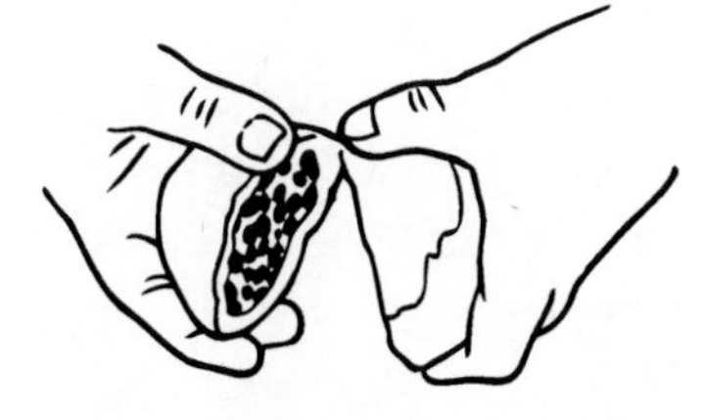

4. Flip the sections open and rub the seeds off the inside of the skin.

5. Soon you will have a bowl of pomegranate seeds. Be careful when you handle the fruit, eat the seeds, or drink the juice, because it stains.

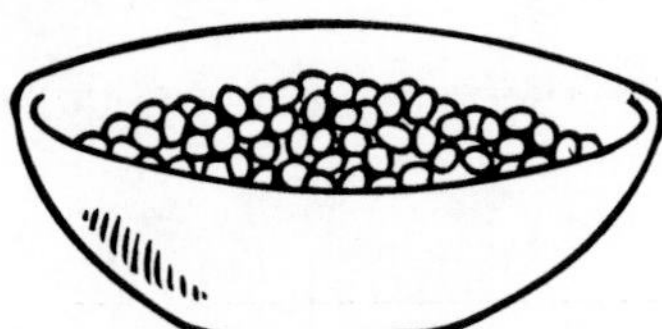

Name

Learn About Mangoes

It can be fun to try a new healthy food. Mangoes are a delicious tropical fruit. They taste a bit like peaches, but the flesh has more fiber. They can be sweet or tart. Mangoes are a *stone fruit,* like a peach or plum, with a single, large seed or "stone" in the center. They grow best in climates that have warm, dry seasons alternating with warm, wet seasons. Different varieties of mango ripen at different times. Mangoes can be harvested from May to September depending on the type.

What does a mango look like?

Shape: Mangoes can be nearly round, oval, or oblong. They are sort of lop-sided in shape.

Size: There are many varieties, from 2" to 10" long, and weighing from a few ounces to 4 or 5 pounds!

Skin: The mango's smooth skin is leathery and waxy. The skin can be green, yellow, orange, or pink. Some mangoes have dark red skin with small yellow, green, or red dots.

Flesh: The flesh of the fruit can be pale yellow to deep orange.

Directions: Use the information above to color the mango. How many different color variations of a mango did your classmates come up with? Which color was the most common? Least common?

How can mangoes be enjoyed?

People eat mangoes as a fresh fruit, sliced, or in salads. Mangoes can also be preserved as jam or eaten as a dried fruit. In other countries, people eat green mangoes or use them in dishes such as green chutney. Some people take the seed out of an unripe mango and roast it for a snack. Researchers have even suggested the fat from the seed be used in chocolate!

Where do mangoes come from?

India grows over half of the world's mango crop. They ship processed and fresh mangoes to countries around the world. Many mangoes are shipped from India to England and France. Fresh mangoes from the Philippines are shipped to other Asian countries. The United States gets its fresh mangoes from Mexico or the state of Florida.

Directions: Answer the questions below. You may need to do some research or look at a map.

1. Which part of the country or world that grows mangoes is closest to where you live?

   ____

2. Based on the text, where do you think the mangoes you buy in the store come from?

   ____

3. Write a sentence about your experience with mangoes. If you have not tasted a mango, what do you think you would like about it? ______________________________

   ____

   ____

Name

Talk About Fruit

Many people like to eat fruit because it is a healthy food choice. It is fun to try new ways to eat it. We can learn about different fruits from our friends.

Directions: Fill in the blanks. Find classmates who have done each of the things listed on the chart. Have that person write his or her name and other information in the correct square. Try to have a different person write in each square.

1. ________________ has tried a yellow tropical fruit. It was a ________________.	**2.** ________________ has had dried fruit. It was ________________.	**3.** ________________ has had apples on a pizza.
4. ________________ thinks starfruit is tasty.	**5.** ________________ has seen an orange tree or a lemon tree.	**6.** ________________ has picked berries. They were ________________. *(name of berry)*
7. ________________ has grown fruit in a garden. He or she grew ________________.	**8.** ________________ has had watermelon at a picnic.	**9.** ________________ has picked fruit from a tree. He or she picked ________________.
10. ________________'s favorite cooked fruit is ________________.	**11.** ________________ likes fruit salad made with ________________ and ________________.	**12.** ________________ has had kiwi fruit. He or she eats it (check box). ☐ cut in half, and scooped out with a spoon. ☐ peeled and sliced.

Name

Think About Vegetables

Vegetables are good for us. They have vitamins and other nutrients to keep us healthy. Vegetables keep our hearts healthy and strong. They also provide:

- **Vitamin C** to help our bodies build strong bones and teeth.
- **Vitamin A** to keep our skin healthy.
- **Folic Acid** to help our bodies make new red blood cells. They carry oxygen to all parts of our bodies.
- **Fiber** to digest the other food we eat.

Directions: Read this list of different vegetables. Check the boxes of the vegetables you have eaten. Put an **X** next to the vegetables you have not tried yet. Circle your three favorite vegetables.

Vegetables

- [ ] artichoke
- [ ] asparagus
- [ ] bean sprouts
- [ ] bok choy
- [ ] broccoli
- [ ] Brussels sprouts
- [ ] cabbage
- [ ] carrots
- [ ] cauliflower
- [ ] celery
- [ ] collard greens
- [ ] corn
- [ ] dry black-eyed peas
- [ ] eggplant
- [ ] endive
- [ ] garbanzo beans
- [ ] iceberg lettuce
- [ ] kale
- [ ] kidney beans
- [ ] leaf lettuce
- [ ] lentils
- [ ] lima beans
- [ ] navy beans
- [ ] olives
- [ ] onions
- [ ] parsnips
- [ ] peas
- [ ] pinto beans
- [ ] potatoes
- [ ] rhubarb
- [ ] romaine lettuce
- [ ] rutabagas
- [ ] snow peas
- [ ] soybeans
- [ ] spinach
- [ ] split peas
- [ ] sweet potatoes
- [ ] taro
- [ ] turnips
- [ ] water chestnuts
- [ ] watercress
- [ ] wax beans
- [ ] white beans

Challenge: Write the names of two vegetables that are new to you.

____________________ ____________________

Research these two vegetables. Write a sentence about each one on the back of this page.

Name

Culinary or Fruit Vegetables

Fruits and vegetables are both healthy foods. Think back to how we define a fruit. *Fruit* is the flower part of a plant in which seeds develop. Many foods we consider vegetables are really fruits because they have seeds inside. We cook or eat these foods as vegetables. We call them "culinary vegetables" or "fruit vegetables."

1. Cross out the vegetables in the grid that do *not* have seeds inside.

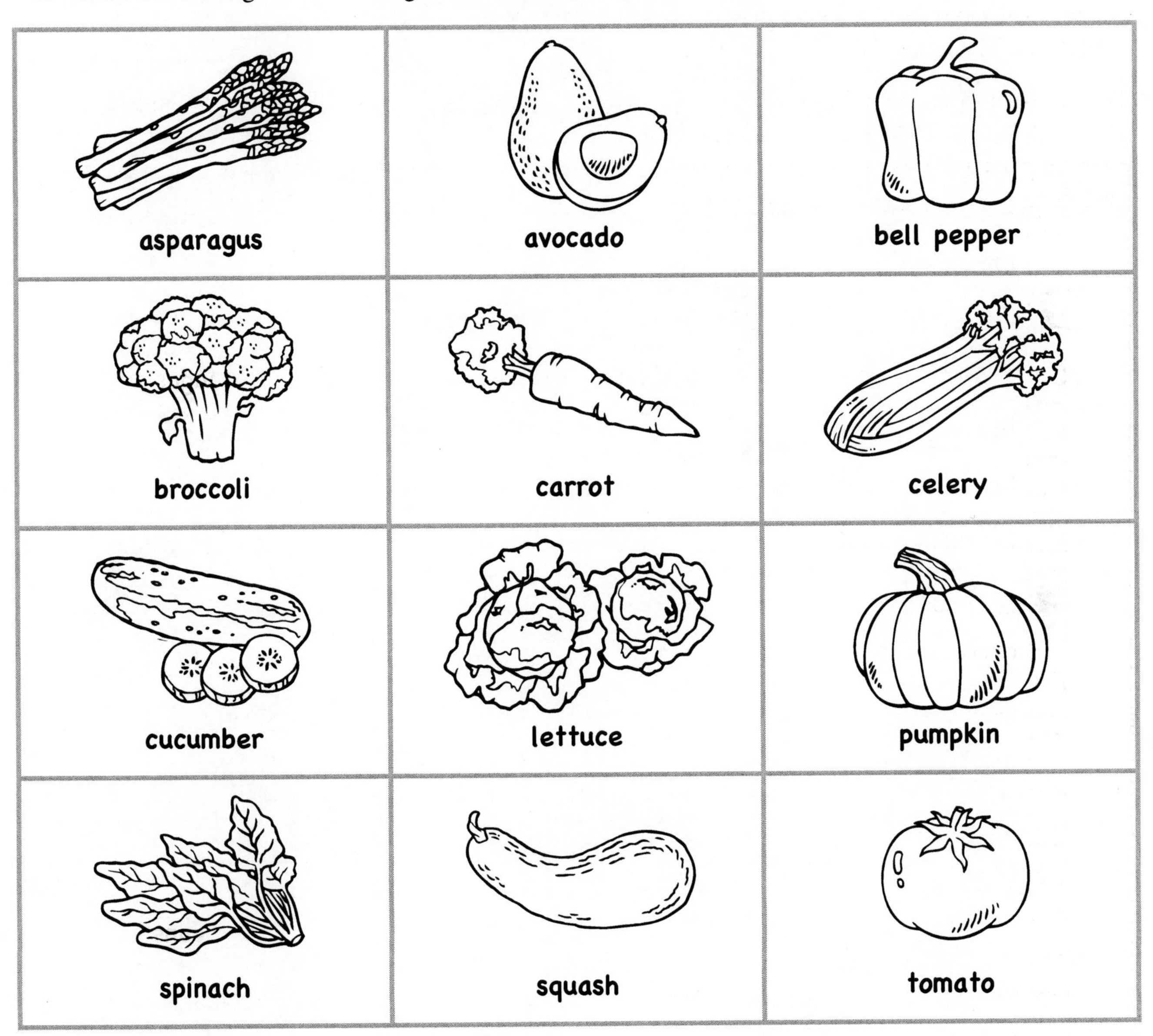

2. List the vegetables that are not crossed out.

______________ ______________ ______________

______________ ______________ ______________

3. What is another name for these vegetables? ______________________________

Name

Plant Parts

Many plants have parts that are safe for people to eat. Any part of a plant we eat that is *not* the fruit we think of as a vegetable. Vegetables can be a plant's *roots, stems, flowers*, or *leaves.* We also eat some *bulbs* and *seeds.*

Directions: Determine into which box each vegetable in the Word Box should go. Some vegetables may go in more than one box. Do we eat the stem, the flowers, the roots, the leaves, the bulbs or the seeds of each vegetable?

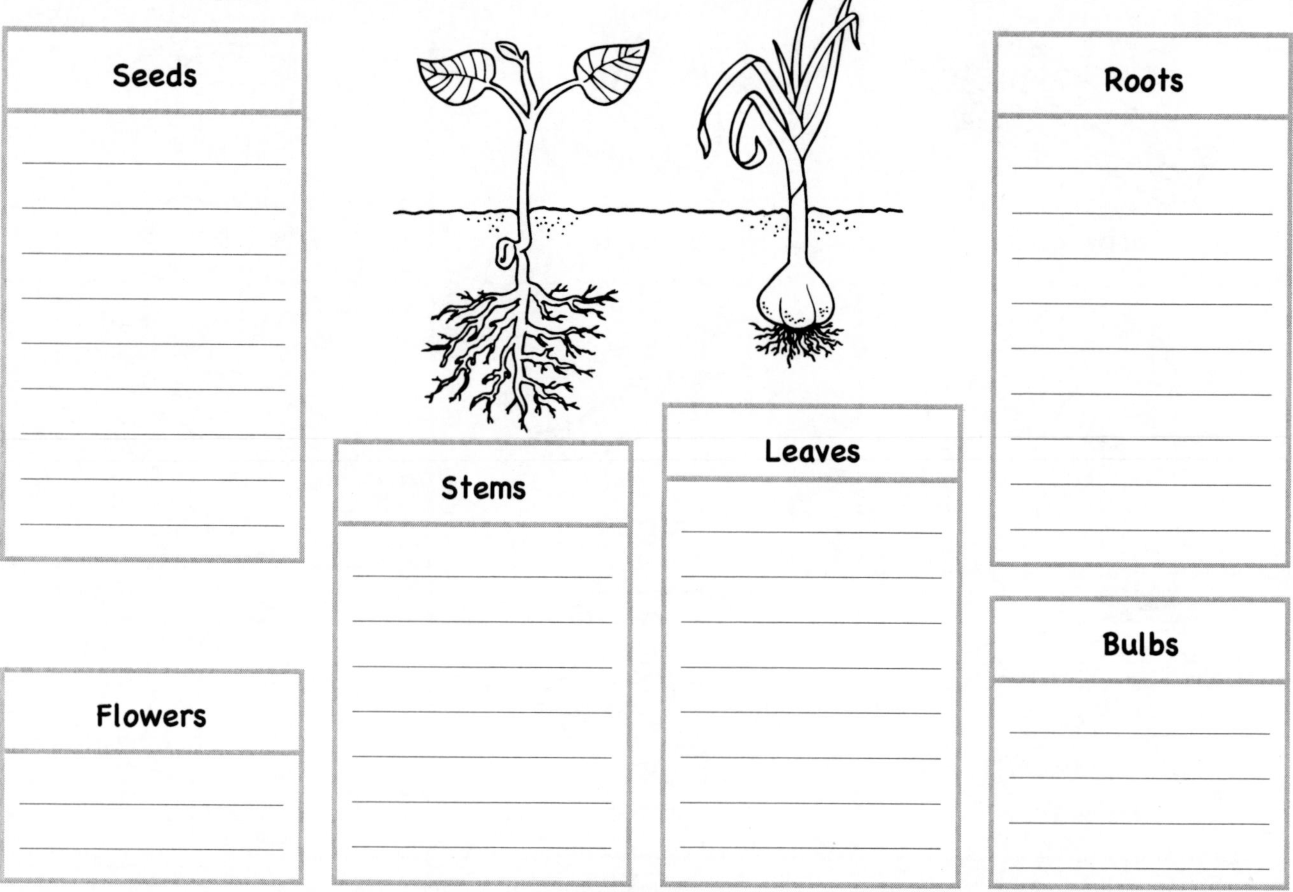

Word Box

asparagus	cauliflower	lima beans	rhubarb
bamboo shoots	celery	onion	rutabaga
beets	collard greens	parsley	spinach
black beans	corn	parsnip	sunflower seeds
bok choy	garlic	peas	sweet potato
broccoli	kale	pinto beans	turnip
Brussels sprouts	kidney beans	potato	water chestnuts
cabbage	leeks	pumpkin seeds	watercress
carrot	lettuce	radish	yam

Name

Where Do Our Vegetables Grow?

Sometimes it's easier to eat healthy foods if they are grown nearby. We might go to a farm or farmer's market to buy fresh produce. Many vegetables grow all around the country. But some states grow most of a particular vegetable sold in stores. The map below provides some examples. Have you tried the vegetable(s) grown there?

Directions: Use the map to answer the questions.

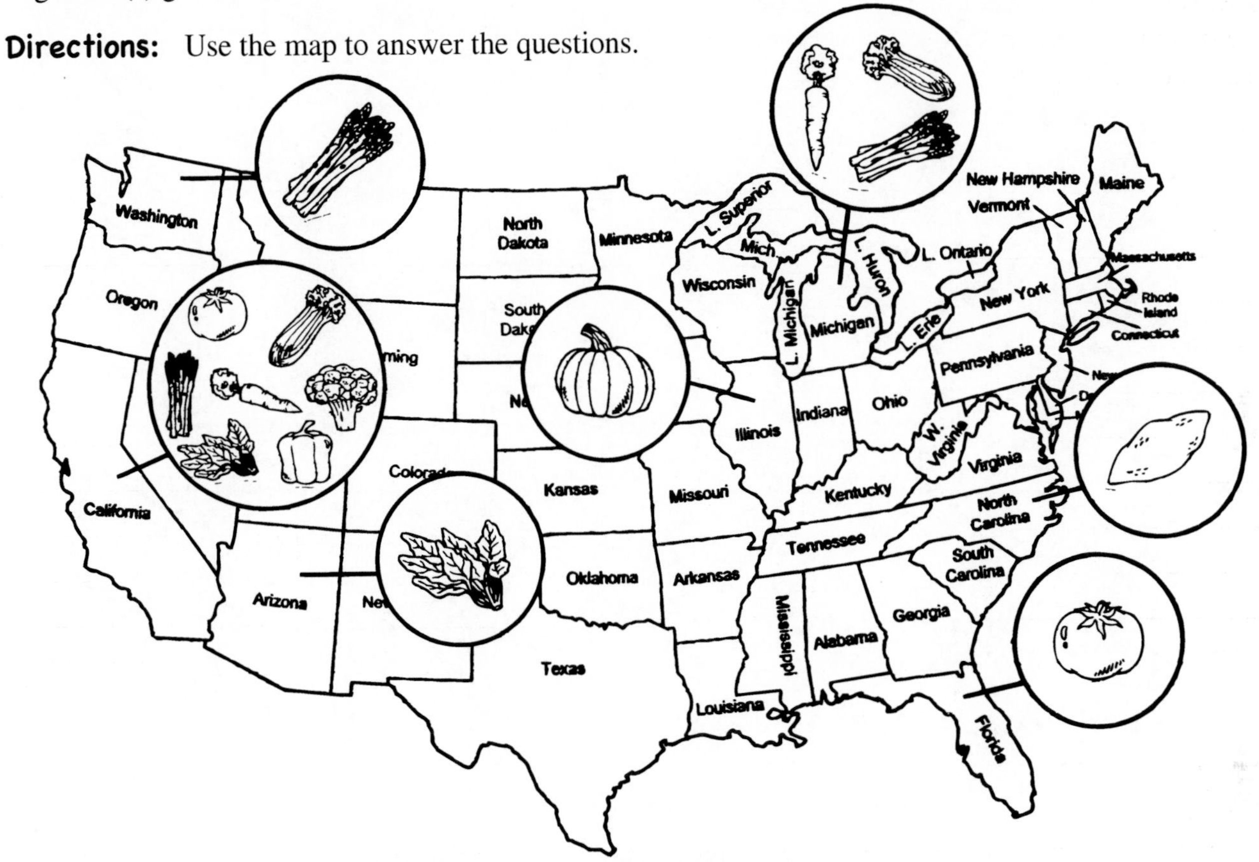

1. Which state provides most of the pumpkin we use for cooking? ______________________

2. Which vegetable is grown in Washington state? ______________________

3. What observation can you make about California from reading the map?

____

____

4. How would this information be useful if you owned a grocery store? ______________________

____

____

5. Which of these vegetables have you tried or would you like to try fresh from the field or a farmer's market? ______________________

Name

Garden to Plate

Let's think about how vegetables get from a farm garden to our plates. Look at the pictures and discuss the steps in the process.

Directions: Create a book or poster. Cut out the pictures, arrange them in order, and describe each step. Add a cover page.

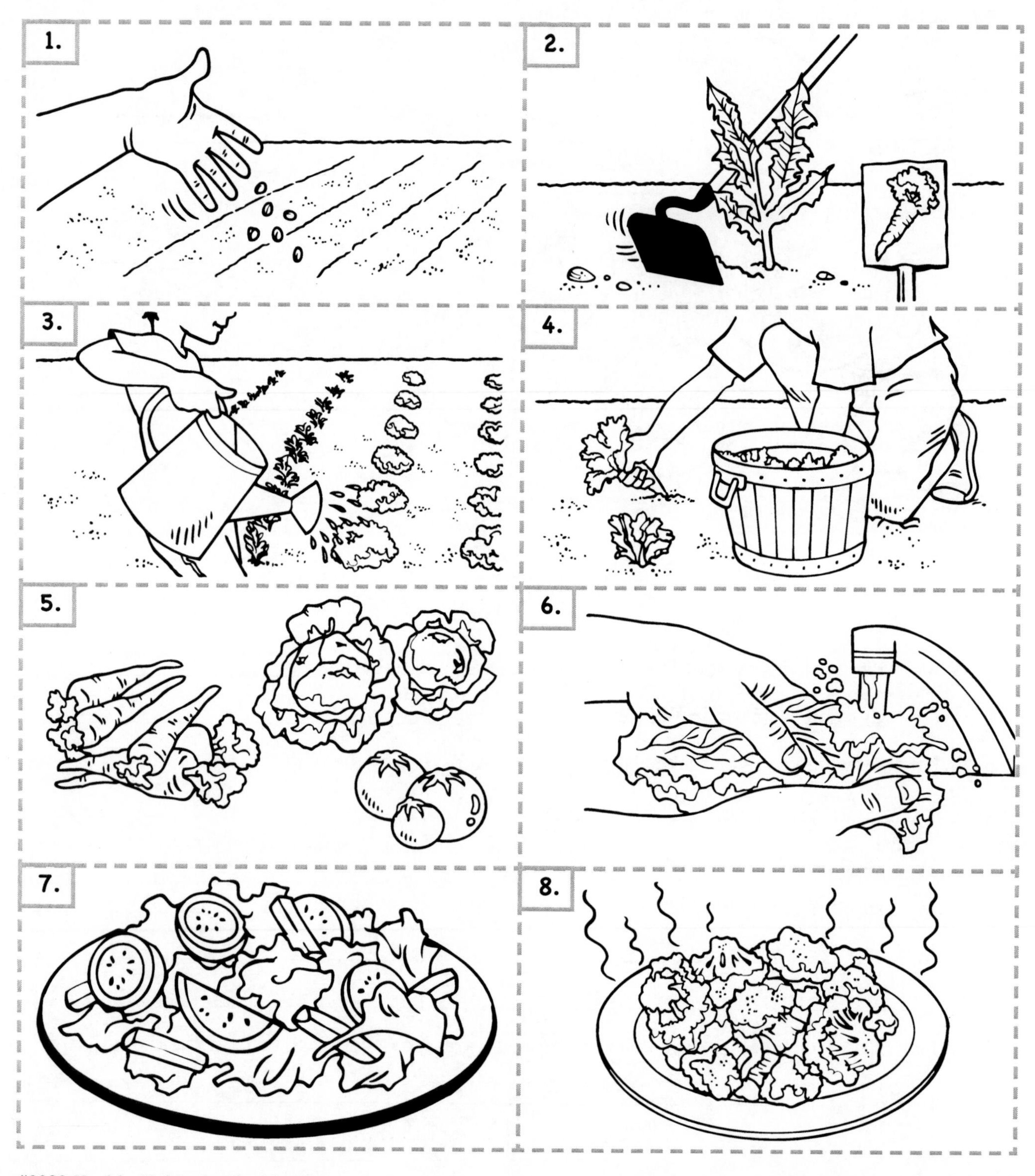

Name

Farm to Store

Think about how vegetables get from a farm to a store. What are the steps in the process? Label each statement with the part of the process it represents: **production**, **processing**, **transportation**, or **distribution**. Cut out the statements and arrange them in order on a separate sheet of paper.

	Vegetables are packaged to ship. ______
	Farmers plant seeds. ______
	Produce is sorted and cleaned. ______
	Machines plow and prepare the soil. ______
	Vegetables are sold in stores. ______
	Vegetables are harvested. ______
	Plants are watered, given nutrients, and weeded. ______
	Vegetables travel by truck to the store. ______

Name

Green Is a Great Color

Green vegetables strengthen our immune system. This means they help keep us from getting sick. The nutrients in green vegetables help blood circulate through our bodies and give us energy. The vitamins in these foods help our blood clot when we are cut.

Many dark green vegetables are from the leaf of the plant.

- **Vitamin C** helps wounds heal.
- **Vitamin A** helps our organs work properly.
- **Vitamin E** helps our immune system, and it keeps our hair and skin healthy.
- **Vitamin K** helps our blood.

Directions: Do some research about the vegetables below. Then, draw a line from the vegetable to its name and color it.

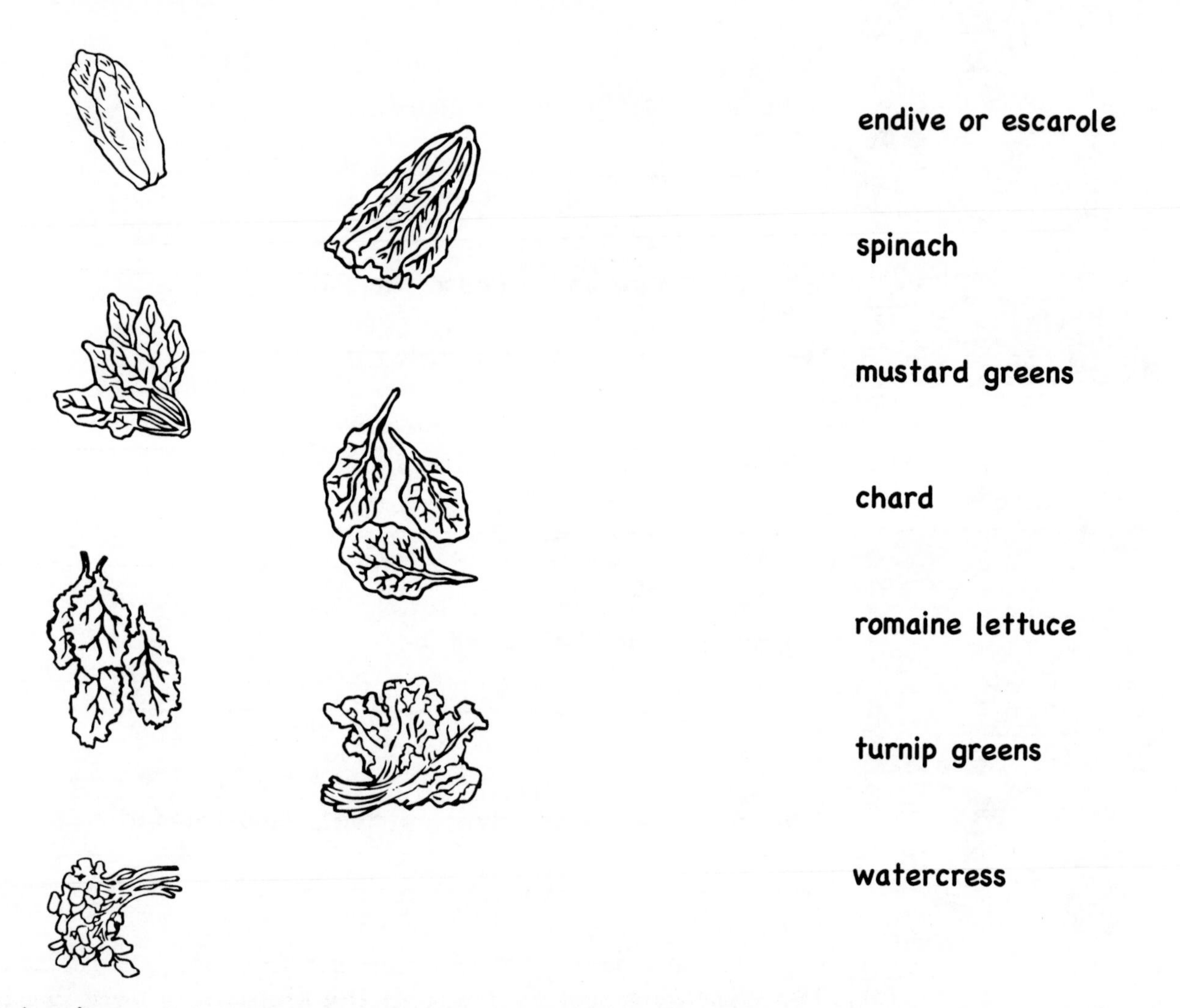

Extensions: Salads are not the only way to eat these vegetables. Ask a family member to chop them up and add them to soup. Blend a few greens with your favorite fruits when you make a smoothie. You won't even be able to taste the greens! Some green vegetables taste good roasted. Have a family member help you roast some broccoli or other greens mixed with other vegetables.

Name

New Vegetables

Look at the vegetables and pictures listed in the Word Box. Circle the ones you have already tried.

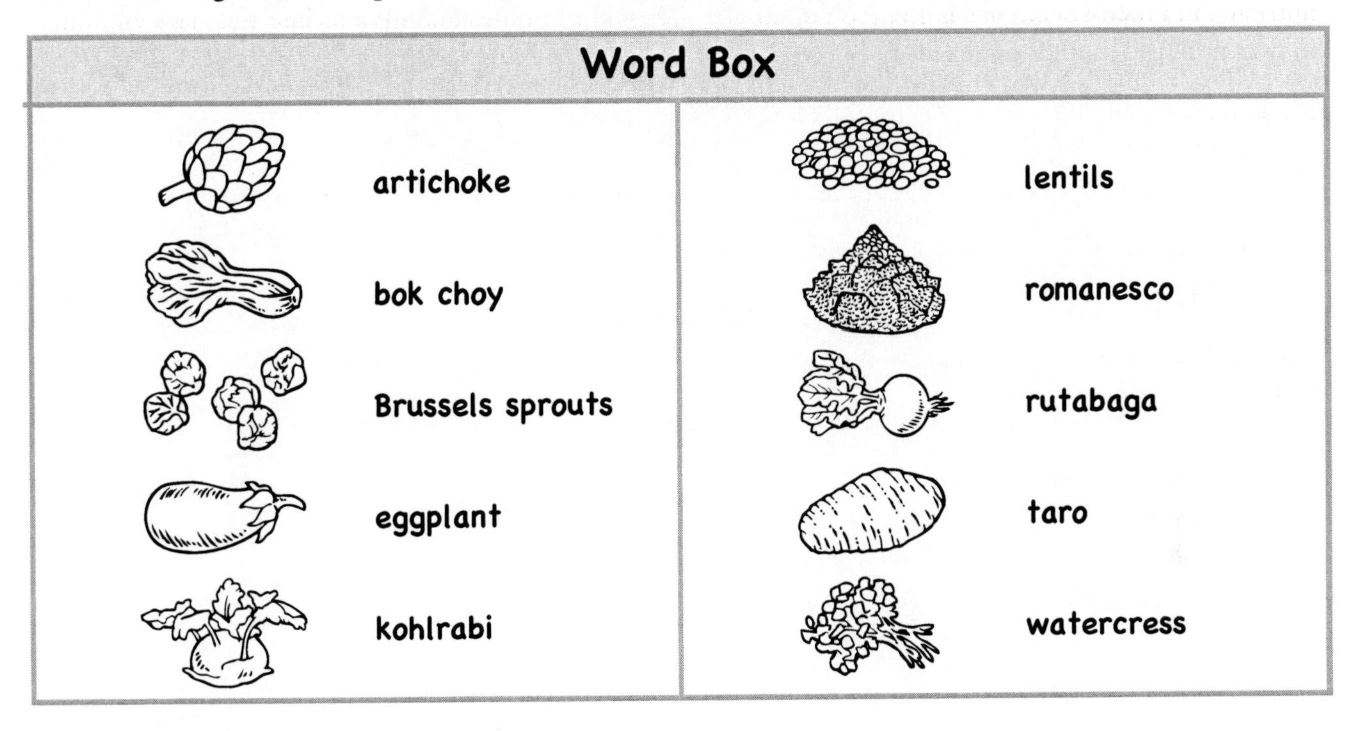

Directions: Match each vegetable to its clue.

1. This vegetable grows just slightly above the ground. ____________________
2. This veggie is named for a city. ____________________
3. This food is a flower bud that has not yet bloomed. ____________________
4. This vegetable is grown in the tropics. ____________________
5. People like to take pictures of this veggie. It is lime green and has a spiral growth pattern.

   ____
6. This vegetable is really a fruit. Plant scientists say it is a berry. ____________________
7. Some people call this Chinese cabbage. ____________________
8. Some people say these greens were part of the first Thanksgiving dinner. ____________________
9. This veggie is a cross between a wild cabbage and a turnip. ____________________
10. These legumes are shaped like contact lenses. ____________________

Which vegetable would you like to try after reading the facts above? ____________________

Why? ____________________

Name

Two Kinds of Peppers

Peppers are healthy "fruit vegetables," and they add flavor to many dishes we eat. Sweet bell peppers and hot chili peppers are in the same plant family. They are also related to tomatoes, potatoes, and eggplant!

Sweet peppers are high in vitamin C and vitamin B-6. They provide fiber. People often eat sweet peppers raw in salads or as a crunchy veggie with dip.

- Bell peppers are sweet peppers that have a mild flavor. Most often, they are green or red. They may also be yellow, orange, or purple. Red bell peppers are the sweetest and green peppers are the least sweet.
- Banana peppers are long, pointed, yellow peppers. They can be sweet or hot (spicy).
- Poblano peppers are dark green, sweet, and mild. They are great for making chile rellenos.
- Sweet cherry peppers look like small red bell peppers and are slightly spicy.

Chili peppers are high in vitamins A, B-6, and C. Most often, they are used to season other foods. A chili pepper triggers sensors in the tongue and skin. It tells your body the temperature is rising. The heat we taste is not just spicy. It really feels as if your mouth is on fire.

- Jalapeños are usually shiny green, but there are also red and purple varieties. They can be hot to very hot. In dried form they are called chipotle.
- Serrano chilies are green. They are smaller and hotter than jalapeños.
- Anaheim chilies are green when fresh. They are red when dried. They may be mild or hot.

Feel the Heat! Chili peppers are rated on the Scoville Heat Unit scale. To find the heat units, scientists dilute a pepper in sugar water. They keep adding sugar until the pepper does not taste hot any more. The more sugar needed, the hotter the pepper ranks on the scale. Below are the Scoville Heat Unit ratings for different five peppers.

Directions: Rank the seven peppers on the chart according to their "heat units." The number 1 will signify the least hot and the number 7 will be for the hottest.

	Scoville Ratings of Peppers	Heat Units
	Anaheim Pepper	1,000–2,500
	Bell Pepper (Mild)	0 (no heat)
	Habañero (Very Hot)	200,000–350,00
	Jalapeño (Hot)	3,500–5,000
	Serrano Green Chili Pepper (Mild)	10,000–23,000
	Banana Pepper	0–500
	Poblano Pepper	1,000–2,000

Name

Think About Whole Grains

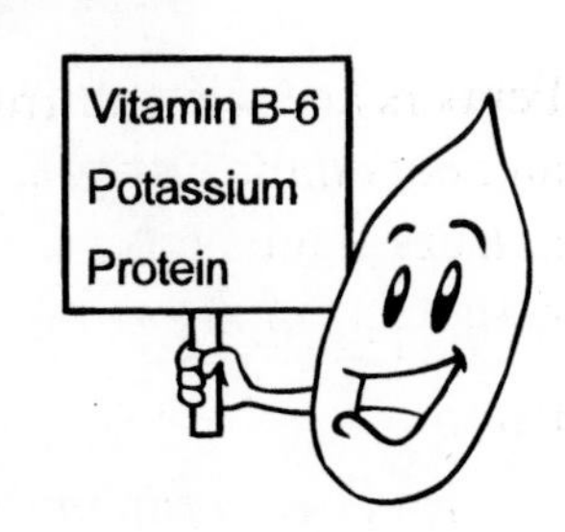

Whole grains are healthy foods. They provide us with carbohydrates. Carbohydrates give us energy. Whole grains also have many vitamins and minerals as well as fiber, protein, and healthy fats. You may be familiar with some whole grains, and some may be new to you.

Directions: Use the whole grains listed in the Word Box to help you unscramble the whole grains on the right. Put a check mark by the ones you have tried.

Word Box
amaranth
barley
brown rice
buckwheat
bulgur
corn
millet
oats
quinoa
rye
sorghum
spelt
wheat
wheat berries

1. athew ________________
2. eiltml ________________
3. estlp ________________
4. homrsug ________________
5. huatbewkc ________________
6. layebr ________________
7. namatrah ________________
8. naqoiu ________________
9. rcno ________________
10. tosa ________________
11. ulrgub ________________
12. wnobr ierc ________________
13. yer ________________
14. hetaw rrseieb ________________

Challenge: On the lines below, write the name of a new whole grain you might try. Research this food. Write what you learn about it and share the information with classmates.

____

____

Name

What Is a Whole Grain?

What is a whole grain? Grains grow in fields. The grain we eat is the seed of the plant. This seed is also called the **kernel**. The **whole grain** has three parts—the *bran*, the *germ*, and the *endosperm.* Each of these parts has important vitamins and other nutrients. Whole grains have all three parts of the kernel left intact.

Directions: Label the diagram below to show all three parts of a whole grain kernel. Look for key words in bold print in the text to help you.

- The **bran** is the multi-layered outer skin of the kernel.
- The **germ** is the embryo of the kernel which can grow into a new plant.
- The **endosperm** surrounds the germ and provides energy for the young plant. It is the largest part of the kernel.

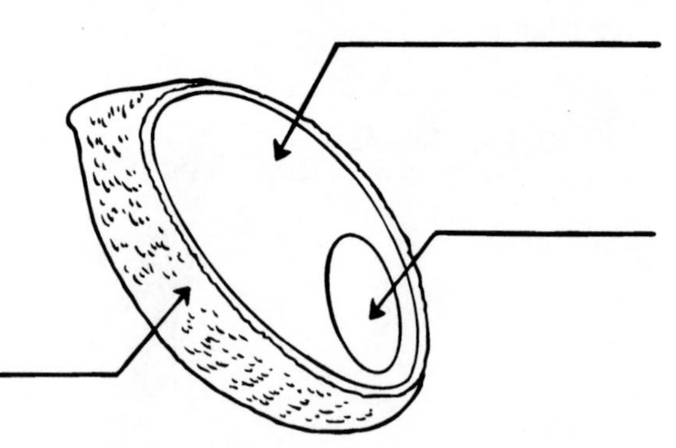

"Images courtesy of Oldways and the Whole Grains Council"

Read food labels to find out if a food has whole grains. There are two easy ways to see if a product is made with whole grains or refined grains. You can tell by looking at the package.

Look for "stamps" like the ones to the left. The top stamp says 100%. It means that the product is 100% whole grain. Each serving has *at least* 16 grams of whole grain.

The bottom stamp does not have the 100% on it. This product is still good for you, but it only has some whole grain and has *at least* 8 grams of whole grain per serving.

If you don't see the stamp, read the ingredients. The word "whole" should be in the ingredients (e.g. **Ingredients**: whole wheat flour, instead of **Ingredients**: wheat flour . . .).

Some grains we eat are "refined." These grains have had the bran and the germ removed. This takes away many important nutrients. During processing, some vitamins and minerals are added back. Whole grains are still healthier for you, though. They provide more protein, carbohydrates, fiber, and other nutrients. These nutrients work together to help us stay healthy. Whole grains are used for flour and in other foods.

Extension: Go to the grocery store with an adult. Bring a pencil and notepad and record the names of products having one of the two seals above. Share the information with classmates and consider creating a display using pictures or packaging.

Name

Types of Corn

Corn is a vegetable. It is also a whole grain. *Corn* grows in a field on tall stalks. Hundreds of years ago, people in South America grew *maize*. This crop was cultivated into the corn we know today. Corn is usually harvested when the stalks are four to six feet tall.

Acres of *dent corn* are grown each year. Some people call this field corn or maize. A dent forms in the top of the kernel as it dries. This type of corn is used to feed animals and make corn syrup, fuel, and biodegradable plastics.

Sweet corn is harvested before it is fully mature. It is sweeter in taste than dent corn. This is the corn we eat as a vegetable. When you eat corn on the cob, you are eating sweet corn. Did you know it has an even number of rows?

Some corn (maize) is soaked in a solution of salt, soda, or lime. Soaking it in lime adds calcium. Soaked kernels of corn make a dish called *hominy*. People eat hominy heated or ground into *grits* (hominy grits) and served with water or milk. Another way to eat hominy is as a soup called posole, popular in Mexico.

If hominy is mashed, it becomes *masa*. Masa is corn that has been soaked in lime water and then mashed up. It is considered a whole grain. People use masa to make *tortillas*.

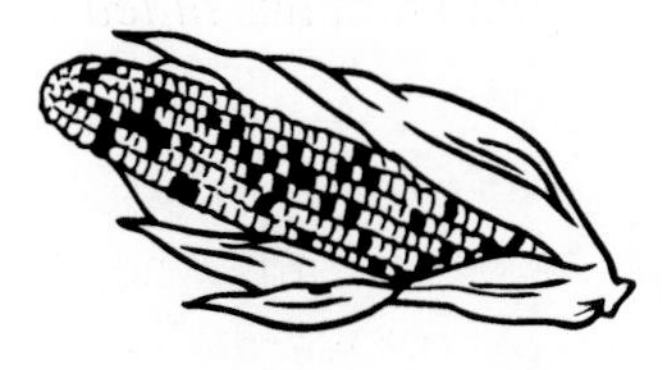

Polenta is a coarse type of corn meal made from *flint* corn. It is boiled to make a porridge that can be eaten. It can also be baked in an oven or grilled. It is also used as a base for other foods, such as chicken or fish.

Popcorn is another type of flint corn. It has a hard hull with a pocket of starch that pops. Steam builds up inside the hull when the corn is heated, and it explodes. There are two basic shapes of popped popcorn: snowflake and mushroom. Which one do you think is bigger and fluffier?

Dried corn can be ground into *cornmeal*. Some cornmeal contains the bran and the germ, so it is a whole grain. We use cornmeal to make corn bread or muffins. It can also be cooked as a hot cereal. Sometimes cornmeal is used to coat fish or other foods before frying or baking.

Name

Corn Review Word Search

Directions: Review the types of corn you read about on the previous page. Then, find each type of corn listed in the Word Box in the word search.

A	N	G	E	R	I	A	L	Q	M	H	D
Q	P	R	H	D	S	H	Y	B	W	E	R
H	O	D	O	A	E	Z	A	U	F	Z	L
B	L	R	M	C	H	G	O	N	T	I	Y
U	E	K	I	L	P	A	R	J	F	A	P
X	N	C	N	B	G	O	M	I	D	M	N
J	T	B	Y	N	C	T	P	F	T	E	R
L	A	H	E	T	U	E	X	I	C	S	O
T	D	E	N	T	C	O	R	N	O	G	C
M	G	I	S	A	L	L	I	T	R	O	T
O	L	Z	B	H	N	H	R	D	N	I	E
F	Q	I	T	R	A	C	K	P	M	H	E
S	A	F	O	G	Y	E	N	A	E	N	W
R	N	C	O	R	N	B	R	E	A	D	S
V	E	S	A	C	W	P	D	T	L	Y	C

Word Box

cornbread
cornmeal
dent corn
flint corn
grits
hominy
maize
masa
polenta
popcorn
sweet corn
tortilla

1. Which type of corn is used for corn on the cob? ____________________
2. Which type of corn is used to feed animals? ____________________
3. Which type of corn is used to make hominy or hominy grits? ____________________
4. What is a popular type of flint corn, often eaten at the movies? ____________________
5. When we grind up dried corn we make ____________________.
6. Tortillas are made from ____________________.

Name

Which Foods Have Whole Grains?

Whole grains have many important vitamins and other nutrients. Whole grains provide fiber. About half of the grains we eat should be whole grains.

How can we be sure our food has whole grains? It can be tricky. Foods that are darker in color are *not always* whole grain. We can read food labels, but sometimes it is confusing. A label might have the words "multi-grain" or "stone-ground." It might say "100% wheat," "cracked wheat," or "bran." These are not usually whole grain foods. Look for labels that have at least one of the words from the whole grain list on page 31.

Whole Grain Spaghetti

Ingredients: whole durum wheat flour

Flour Tortillas

Ingredients: enriched bleached wheat flour, water, vegetable shortening, oil, leavening, salt, preservatives

Raisin Cereal

Ingredients: whole grain wheat, raisins, corn bran, sugar, whole grain rice, whole grain oats, wheat bran, glycerin, corn syrup, brown sugar, salt, honey, corn starch, cinnamon, preservatives

Whole Wheat Bread

Ingredients: whole wheat flour, water, wheat gluten, wheat bran, corn syrup, oil, molasses, salt, yeast, honey, wheat germ

Directions

1. Read the ingredients taken from the labels of the four whole-wheat products above. Underline the ingredients that tell you whether or not the food is whole grain.

2. Which food is not a whole grain product? ____________________

   How do you know? ____________________

3. Which foods can be made with grains other than wheat? ____________________

   ____

Name

Whole Grains Every Day

Most people already eat grains every day. When possible, choose foods that have *whole* grains like whole wheat bread, whole wheat tortillas, and wild or brown rice. Other foods have *refined* grains. White bread, white rice, and white flour are refined grains.

Refined grains have been milled (processed) so they no longer have the bran and the germ of the kernel. In this process, fiber, iron, and the vitamins are removed. If you do eat refined grains foods, look for the word "enriched" on the label. This means that some vitamins and iron have been added back in but not fiber. What are some choices you can make to eat whole grains instead of refined grains?

Directions: Work with a partner. Brainstorm ways you can eat more whole grains every day. Write your ideas on the graphic organizer.

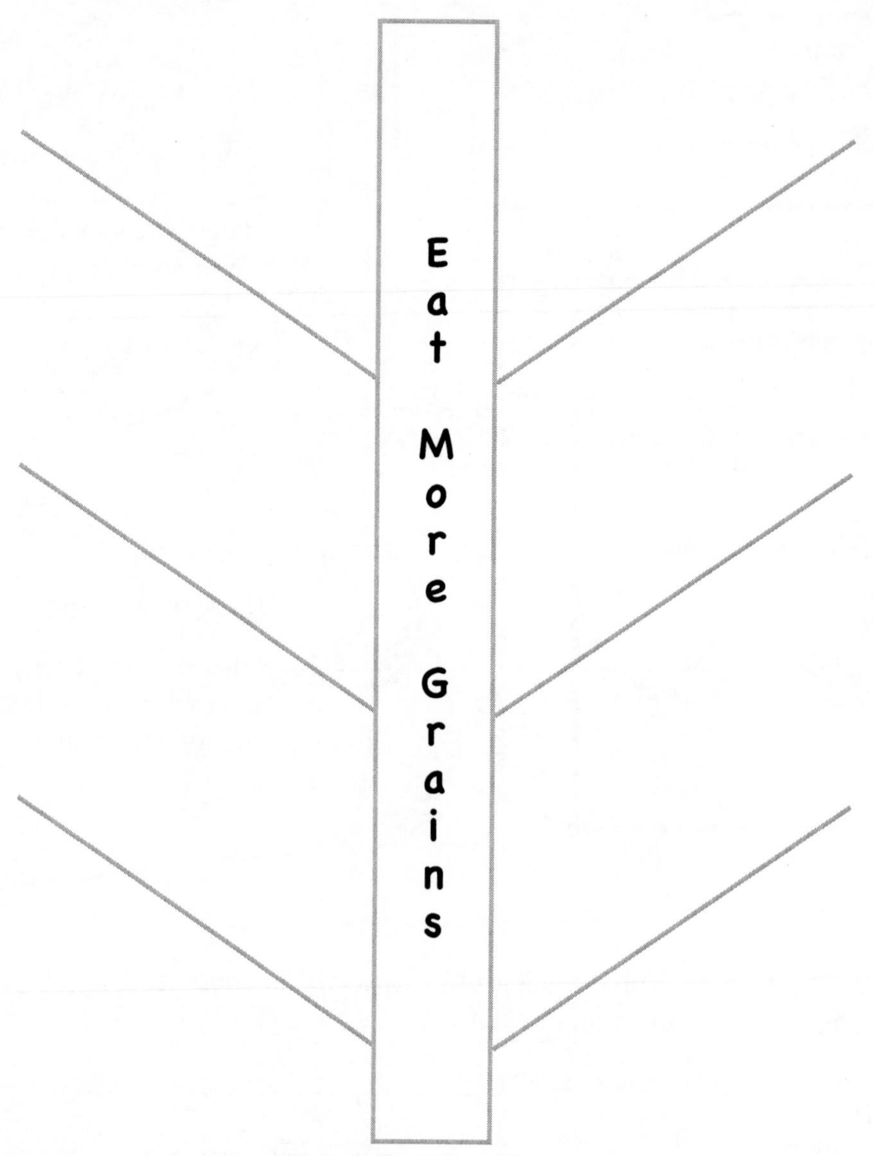

Challenge: Make a poster to help others remember to eat whole grains. Include the ideas from your notes and your discussion with your partner. Make your poster interesting so others will want to read it.

Name

Think About Dairy Foods

Milk and cheese are healthy foods. They are part of the dairy food group. These foods give us calcium, vitamins and minerals, and protein. Dairy foods help us build strong bones and teeth. We can choose low-fat milk and cheese to keep our hearts and blood vessels healthy.

Directions: Check the dairy foods you have tried. Put an **X** in front of the ones you have not tasted. Circle one or two dairy foods you would like to try.

Dairy	
☐ buttermilk	☐ Greek yogurt
☐ cheddar cheese	☐ milk
☐ condensed milk	☐ mozzarella cheese
☐ cottage cheese	☐ parmesan cheese
☐ dried or powdered milk	☐ pudding
☐ evaporated milk	☐ ricotta cheese
☐ frozen yogurt	☐ Swiss cheese

1. Write about an experience you have had eating a dairy food. ______________________

____

____

2. Explain why you would like to try the foods that you circled. ______________________

____

____

3. Write a question you have about one of these dairy foods. ______________________

____

4. Find the answer to the question you wrote in #3.

____

____

Teacher Note: Butter has no calcium and is not considered a dairy food, even though it is made from milk. Soymilk, which is a plant-based product, is considered a dairy product when it is fortified with calcium.

Name

How Do We Get Our Milk?

You may have read about the days when farmers milked cows by hand. The milk would go into a clean pail, and he or she would take the pail of milk to the house. The milk would be poured into glasses right from the pail and served for dinner! In most places, it's a little different now. You probably pour your milk from a container that you get out of the refrigerator. Someone in your household bought that milk at a store. And the cow is probably not in the field next door! So how does our milk get from the cows to us?

Directions for pages 38 and 39

1. Read and cut out the statements below. They describe the process of getting milk, but they are not in order.
2. Cut out the pictures (page 39) and use them to put the statements below in the correct order. Number the statements in the correct order.
3. Combine the statements and the pictures to create a book or poster showing the process of bringing milk from the cow to the store. **You will have more than one statement for two of the pictures.**

How Do We Get Our Milk?

MILK

______	Milk is put into jugs or containers.
______	Milk is homogenized to prevent any remaining fat particles from rising to the top of the milk and forming a cream layer. This step gives milk a more consistent texture and appearance.
______	Trucks transport milk from farm to factory and workers test the milk again.
______	People buy milk at the store.
______	Milk is tested by farmers.
______	Milk is put into refrigerated tanks immediately to prevent the growth of harmful bacteria.
______	Cows graze on farms. They are fed grains. Their bodies process this food to produce milk.
______	Cows are milked with milking machines.
______	Trucks transport the milk containers to stores for purchase.
______	Milk is pasteurized (heated) to kill harmful bacteria.

Name

How Do We Get Our Milk? *(cont.)*

1. Cows graze.

2. Cows are milked.

3. Milk is refrigerated and tested.

4. Milk is transported to be processed.

5. The milk is tested again.

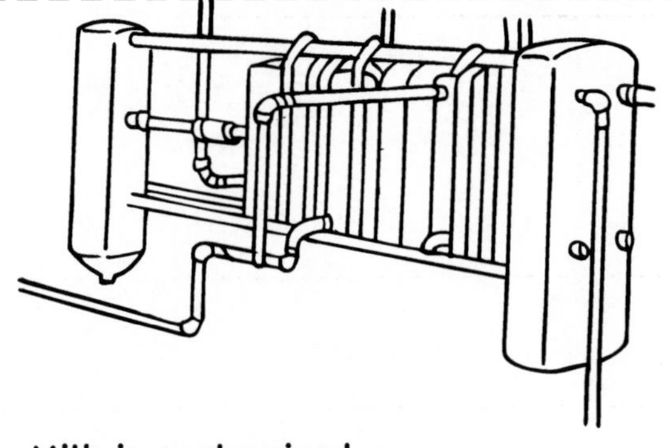

6. Milk is pasteurized.

7. Milk is homogenized.

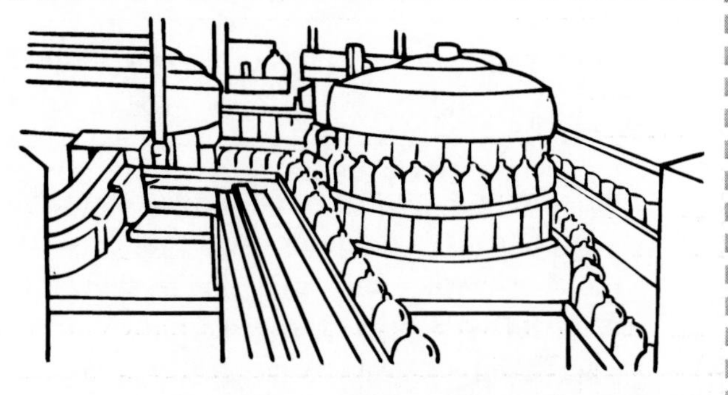

8. Milk is put in containers to be purchased.

Name

What's the Difference?

Yogurt is a healthy dairy food. You may have seen different kinds of yogurt at the store. There are two main kinds, Greek yogurt and "regular" yogurt. What's the difference between the two?

Greek yogurt is strained yogurt. The straining removes excess whey, lactose, and sugar. The resulting yogurt is thicker. If you compared the same amount of Greek yogurt and regular yogurt, you would find that the Greek yogurt has more protein. It has fewer carbohydrates and is lower in sugar, too. Some people think Greek yogurt is creamier but not as sweet as regular yogurt.

Most yogurt has live bacterial cultures. This helps keep our digestive systems healthy. Both types of yogurt provide calcium and can be low-calorie foods.

No matter which kind of yogurt you choose, look for brands of yogurt with less added sugar. Read labels to see if the yogurt is low fat. Check to see that other ingredients like cornstarch have not been added.

1. Think about the ways regular and Greek yogurt are the same. How are they different? Write your observations in the Venn diagram below.

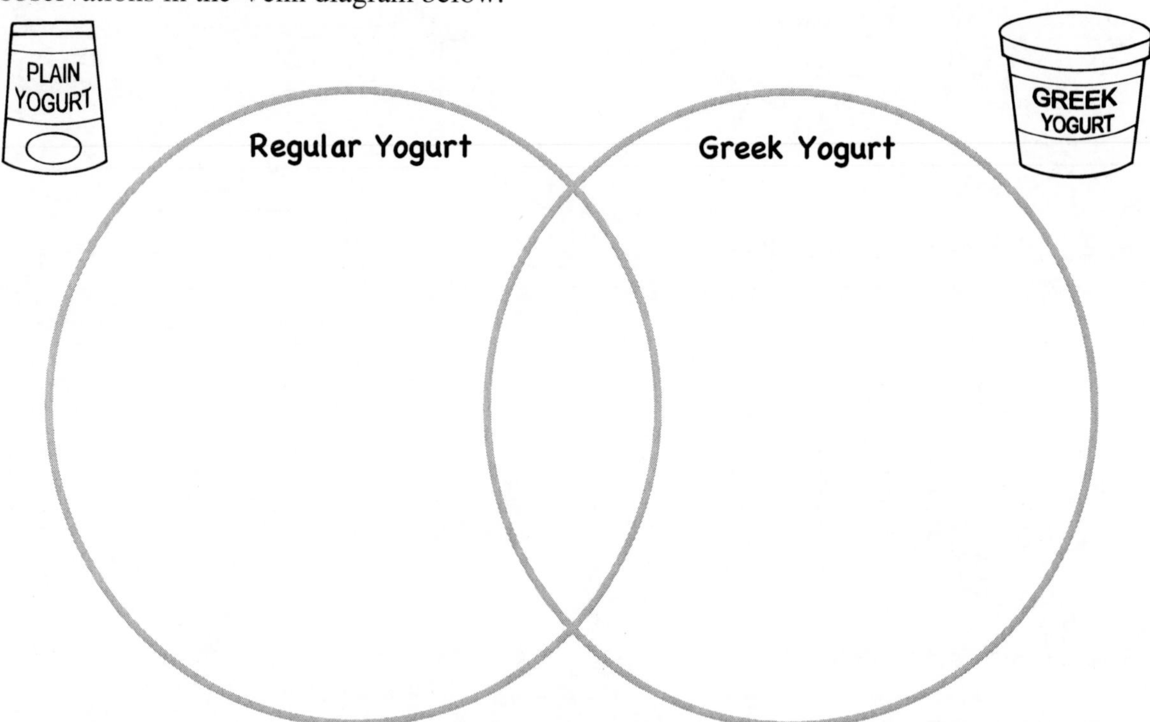

2. Which yogurt do you prefer? **Greek Yogurt** **Regular Yogurt**

   Why?____

Either kind of yogurt can be a healthy food choice. Try these tips to add more yogurt to your diet:

- Use yogurt as a dip for raw vegetables. Add seasonings such as garlic, dill, or parsley to spice it up a bit.
- Substitute yogurt for sour cream on tacos and dips.
- Mix fruit with low-fat yogurt for a tasty breakfast.
- Use Greek yogurt as a spread instead of cream cheese, mayonnaise, or butter which all have a higher fat content.

Name

Eating Dairy Foods

Directions: Brainstorm some ways to eat dairy foods. Use the Word Box at the bottom of the page to help you complete the sentences. You may use some words more than once.

1. I can have ____________________ in a bowl of ____________________ .
2. I can make a ____________________ for vegetables out of ____________________ .
3. I can put a slice of ____________________ on a ____________________ for lunch.
4. I can make a ____________________ out of fruit and ____________________ .
5. I can stir some ____________________ into ____________________ for a tasty breakfast or lunch.
6. I can drink a ____________________ of ____________________ at dinner.
7. I can add ____________________ to my ____________________ .
8. I can have ____________________ with whole grain ____________________ instead of a sandwich at lunch.
9. Two of my favorite ways to eat dairy foods are ____________________ and ____________________.

   I like these foods because ____.

Word Box		
cereal	fruit	smoothie
cheese	glass	taco
crackers	milk	tortilla
dip	sandwich	yogurt

Name

Think About Protein Foods

We get protein from meat, poultry, and seafood. Beans, peas, and eggs are protein foods, and so are nuts and seeds. It is important to get enough protein each day. Protein helps:

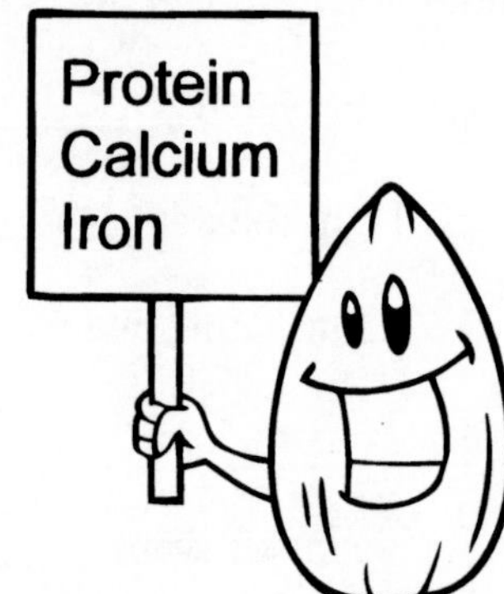

- build, maintain, and replace tissues in our bodies. These tissues are found in bones, muscles, and organs. Building and maintaining these tissues helps us move and breathe.
- our bodies make red blood cells, which carry oxygen to all parts of our bodies.
- our immune system protect us against disease and infection. It helps us stay healthy and well.
- give us energy.

Directions: Here is a list of protein foods. Many of these you may already eat, but some may be new to you. Put a check by the foods you have eaten. Put an **X** in boxes next to foods you have not tried yet. Circle your three favorite protein foods.

Protein		
☐ almonds	☐ ground chicken	☐ pinto beans
☐ beef	☐ ground lamb	☐ pork
☐ bison	☐ ground pork	☐ pumpkin seeds
☐ black beans	☐ ground turkey	☐ rabbit
☐ black-eyed peas	☐ ham	☐ sesame seeds
☐ cashews	☐ hazelnuts	☐ shellfish
☐ chicken	☐ kidney beans	☐ soybeans
☐ chickpeas (garbanzo beans)	☐ lamb	☐ split peas
☐ duck	☐ lima beans	☐ sunflower seeds
☐ eggs	☐ navy beans	☐ tuna
☐ fish	☐ nuts	☐ turkey
☐ goose	☐ peanuts	☐ veal
☐ ground beef	☐ pecans	☐ venison
	☐ pistachios	☐ walnuts

Challenge: Do some research and learn about two protein foods that are new to you. Explain why would you like to try each of these foods. Use the back of the page to answer.

Name

Beef Is a Source of Protein

Lean beef gives us protein. Protein is an important nutrient. Beef protein combines nutrients in a way our bodies can use. These nutrients keep our red blood cells and nerves healthy. Protein helps us build new cells and make enzymes we need to digest our food. Basically, protein keeps our bodies running.

Red meat like beef has iron in a form that our bodies can absorb easily. Iron helps the blood carry oxygen to the body's cells. Beef has vitamins and minerals, too. It is best to eat lean red meat that has not been processed too much. This helps us get the important nutrients without getting added chemicals or fillers our bodies do not need.

Directions: Use the clues on page 44 to fill in the crossword puzzle.

Word Box	
angus	heifer
beef	lean
bovine	longhorn
bull	range
calf	roast
cattle	ruminant
cow	steak
hamburger	steer

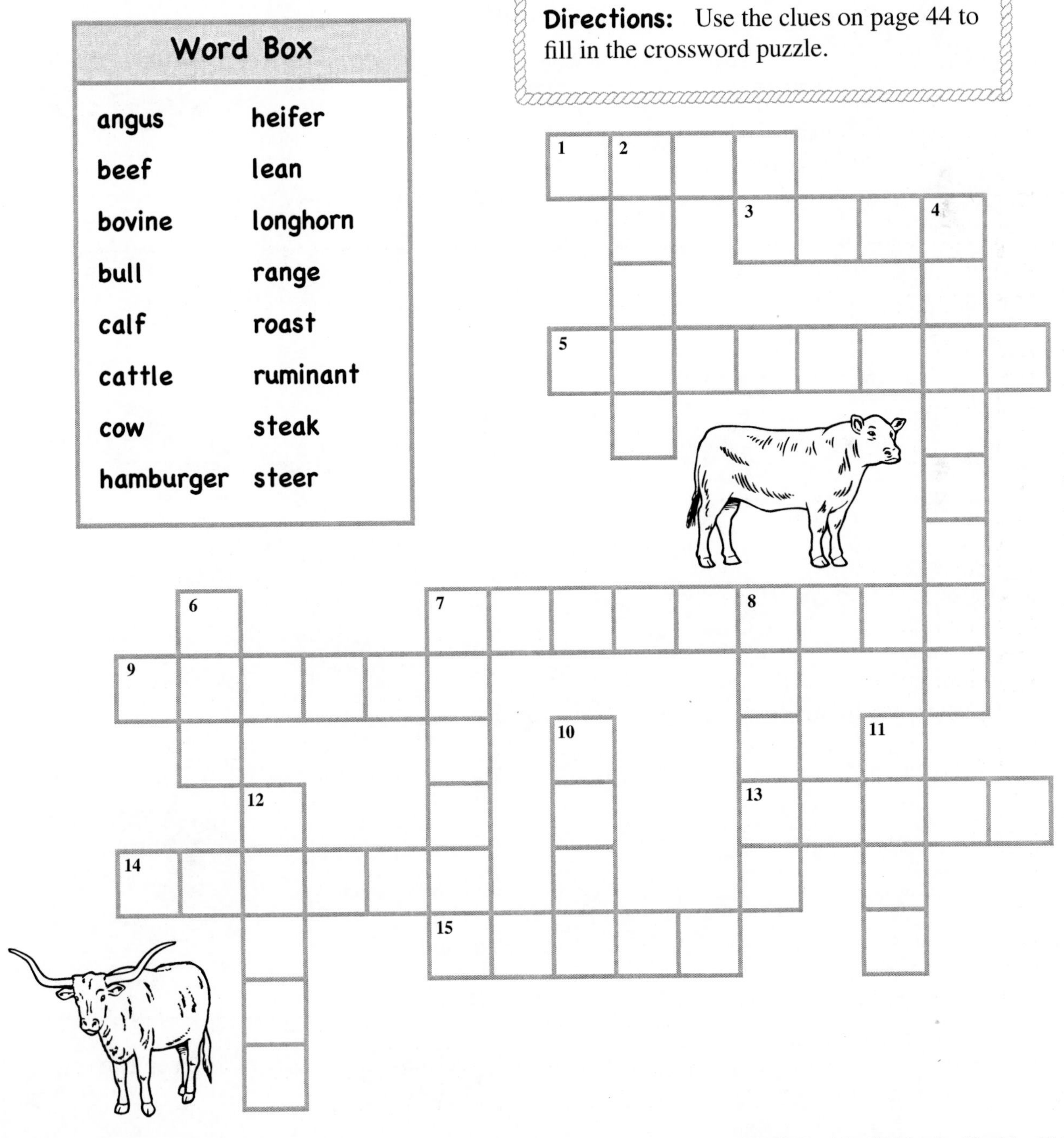

Name

Beef Is a Source of Protein *(cont.)*

Directions: Use the Word Box on page 43 and a dictionary to fill in the blanks and learn more about beef. Then fill in the crossword puzzle on page 43 using the answers from this page.

Across

1. A _____ _____ _____ _____ is a young male or female cow less than one year of age.
3. A _____ _____ _____ _____ is a mature male bovine that can reproduce.
5. A _____ _____ _____ _____ _____ _____ _____ _____ is an animal that eats plants and converts them into meat or milk that humans can eat.
7. A _____ _____ _____ _____ _____ _____ _____ _____ _____ is made from ground beef.
9. The term _____ _____ _____ _____ _____ _____ refers to cattle.
13. A _____ _____ _____ _____ _____ is a thick slice of beef cut across the muscle grain.
14. Cows, bulls, and steers have hooves and are raised for food or for their hides. They are also known as _____ _____ _____ _____ _____ _____
15. Cattle graze on an area of open grassy land called a _____ _____ _____ _____ _____ .

Down

2. _____ _____ _____ _____ _____ is a breed of cattle known for tender beef.
4. The earliest breed of cattle raised for beef in the United States is the Texas _____ _____ _____ _____ _____ _____ _____ _____ .
6. A mature female that has produced a calf is called a _____ _____ _____.
7. A female cow over one year old that has not had a calf is called a _____ _____ _____ _____ _____ _____ .
8. _____ _____ _____ _____ _____ beef is cooked in a hot oven.
10. Meat that is _____ _____ _____ _____ has little or no fat.
11. The meat that comes from the muscle of an adult cow is called _____ _____ _____ _____.
12. A _____ _____ _____ _____ _____ is an adult male cow raised as beef for people to eat.

Name

Fish—Protein and Good Fat

Fish is another good source of protein. It provides about the same amount of protein per serving as other types of meat. Fish is low in calories and fat. It also has omega-3 fatty acids, a healthy type of fat. This makes fish a healthy way to get protein.

There are two kinds of fat: healthy fat and unhealthy fat. Most fish is low in unhealthy fat. Some kinds of fish, such as salmon or tuna, are high in omega-3 fatty acids. That might sound bad, but that type of fat in fish helps keep our heart and blood vessels healthy.

Some animals that live in the water are called *shellfish.* They have a shell, or exoskeleton. Many shellfish are also good to eat in limited amounts. They provide protein and healthy fat in our diets.

1. Read the list of types of fish and shellfish people eat. Circle the shellfish in the list.

Word Box			
catfish	crayfish	salmon	snapper
clam	halibut	scallop	swordfish
cod	herring	sea bass	trout
crab	lobster	shrimp	tuna

2. Find each fish and shellfish in the word search.

S	C	A	L	L	O	P	S	D	L
B	W	L	E	C	F	H	N	Y	O
H	C	O	R	T	R	M	A	G	B
S	O	A	R	I	F	T	P	N	S
I	B	O	M	D	O	C	P	I	T
F	U	P	G	R	F	T	E	R	E
T	U	N	A	K	U	I	R	R	R
A	S	E	A	B	A	S	S	E	G
C	E	G	I	R	G	M	B	H	P
S	A	L	M	O	N	Y	R	N	A
N	A	R	L	S	M	A	L	C	S
H	S	I	F	Y	A	R	C	W	B

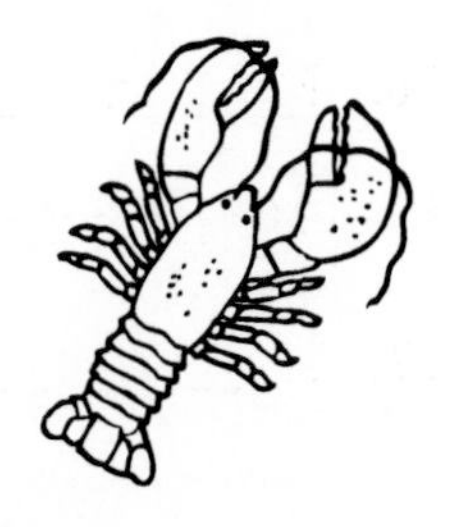

Name

Legumes for Protein and More!

Beans and peas are unique foods. They are legumes, which are plants with seeds that grow in pods. Peas, beans, lentils, and peanuts are all legumes. These foods are in the vegetable group, but they are also in the protein group. They provide protein and nutrients similar to those found in meat. They are also good sources of fiber and potassium. These nutrients are found in many vegetables.

Directions: Use the clues in the box below to find the names of common legumes. You may need to do some research.

① L _ _ t _ _ _

② c h _ _ _ _ _ E _ _

③ G _ _ _ _ _ z _ _ _ _ n _

④ _ _ _ _ U _ _

⑤ M _ _ g B _ a _ _

⑥ _ E _ _

⑦ B _ _ _ S _ _ _ _ _ _

Legume Clues

1. ______________________ are used in soups.

2. ______________________ are used to make hummus and in salads.

3. Another name for the answer in #2 is ______________________.

4. ______________________ are also called "groundnuts" because they grow underground.

5. ______________________ are small green, yellow, or black legumes often used to make bean sprouts or soups.

6. ______________________ are green, round, and come in pods. They can be cooked or eaten fresh from the garden.

7. ______________________ are great on salads or sandwiches.

Name

Nuts About Protein

Nuts are protein foods that grow on trees. There are many different kinds of nuts. Nuts are low in fat and help keep our hearts healthy. They help our blood vessels stay healthy and may prevent blood clots. Nuts have healthy types of fat, fiber, and vitamin E.

Nuts make a good snack food. They are easy to take with you and eat when you are away from home. Check the serving size for the type of nuts you like to eat. One serving of nuts can be anywhere from 5 to 50 nuts, depending on the variety. Sometimes even the snack-size bags have more than one serving.

Directions: Match each nut to its name.

almond

brazil nuts

cashew

hazelnut

macadamia nuts

pistachios

walnuts

Are Peanuts Nuts?

Some people call peanuts "groundnuts." This is because they grow underground. Peanuts are actually *legumes*. They are an edible seed that grows in a pod. A peanut plant or bush develops flowers near the base of the plant. The flowers lose their petals. Then, the budding "peg" grows down away from the plant to the soil. The way they grow is similar to legumes. Peanuts give us protein and fiber and are good sources of vitamins B and E, and magnesium. We use peanuts in cooking and eating, more like a nut.

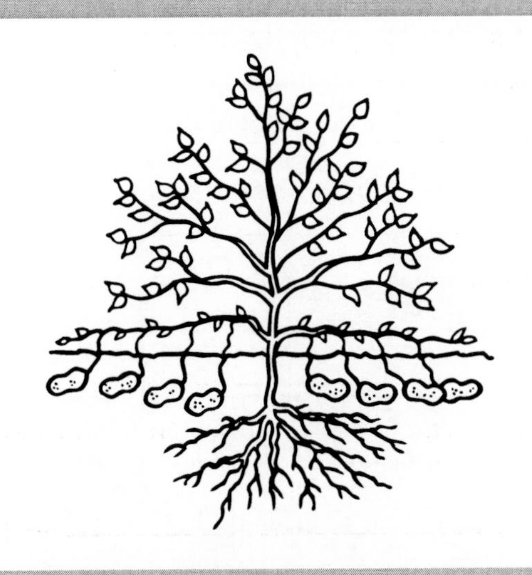

Name

Making Healthy Food Choices

Many people in our country do not eat enough fruits or vegetables.

Directions: Here is a list of ways to eat more fruits and vegetables. Check the ways you have tried and then answer the questions below.

- ☐ Picture your meal on a plate. Do you have fruits and vegetables on half the plate? You should!
- ☐ Keep fruits and vegetables handy for snacking.
- ☐ Ask if your family can try a new fruit or vegetable you have learned about.
- ☐ Add fruit to your cereal.
- ☐ Enjoy hot vegetable soup on a cold day.
- ☐ Add vegetables to a tortilla wrap.
- ☐ Dip vegetables in a healthy dip, such as hummus or yogurt.
- ☐ Experiment with different vegetables on sandwiches. Try avocado, bean sprouts, or cucumber. How about green pepper, lettuce, or tomato? What else might be good on a sandwich?
- ☐ Add different vegetables to your salad of leafy greens.
- ☐ Eat vegetables prepared in different ways. If you don't care for a vegetable cooked, try eating it raw. Do the reverse with vegetables you have only eaten cooked.

1. Describe your favorite way to add vegetables to your day. Share your ideas with a friend.

____

____

2. What is one new way you would like to try to have fruits or vegetables?

____

____

Challenge: Divide into three groups and brainstorm ways to make good food choices about the other food groups—**Grains, Dairy**, and **Protein**. Combine your ideas to fill in the chart.

Grains	Dairy	Protein
____________	____________	____________
____________	____________	____________
____________	____________	____________
____________	____________	____________

Name

Vitamins and Minerals Chart

Vitamins and minerals help keep us healthy. We get these nutrients from the foods we eat. Different foods have different nutrients, so we eat foods from each food group each day. This helps us get all the vitamins and minerals we need.

Directions: Read the chart to learn how different vitamins and minerals help us stay healthy. Then, answer the questions on pages 50 and 51.

Nutrient	Health Benefits	Foods
Vitamin A	healthy hair, skin, and eyes; helps make white blood cells to fight germs	apricots, broccoli, carrots, cheese, milk, spinach, sweet potatoes
Vitamin B	healthy blood; helps our bodies use energy from food	chicken, eggs, fish, lean meat, milk, whole grains
Vitamin C	healthy teeth, gums, muscles; protects us from infection and helps us heal	broccoli, Brussels sprouts, cabbage, grapefruit, kiwi fruit, oranges, peppers, strawberries, tomatoes
Vitamin D	strong bones and teeth; helps our bodies use calcium	eggs, fish, milk
Vitamin E	healthy blood, eyes, liver, lungs, and skin	avocado, eggs, leafy green vegetables, nuts, peanut butter, seeds, whole grains
Vitamin K	helps blood clot, which allows wounds to stop bleeding	dark green leafy vegetables, cabbage, cauliflower, eggs, meat, milk, peas, yogurt
Folic Acid	aids red blood cell health	dark green leafy vegetables, dried beans and peas
Calcium	strong bones and teeth; muscles; keeps cells healthy; helps blood clot, which allows wounds to stop bleeding	citrus fruits, dark green leafy vegetables, dried beans and peas, milk
Phosphorus	helps our bodies use energy from food; keeps cells healthy	chicken, dried beans and peas, eggs, fish, meat, milk
Magnesium	strong bones; helps our bodies use energy from food; keeps our nerves healthy (allows nerves to send messages back and forth between the brain and the body to keep us safe)	nuts, raw leafy green vegetables, seeds, whole grains
Potassium	healthy muscles, cells, and nerves; helps body use energy from food	bananas, dried beans and peas, meat, orange juice, peanut butter, potatoes
Iron	healthy blood cells and muscles; helps blood carry oxygen to cells	dried beans and peas, dried fruits, eggs, leafy green vegetables, red meat, potatoes

Name

Vitamins

Directions: Fill in the missing words as you read. You may use some words more than once. Do some research and check the chart on page 49 for more vitamin information.

1. Our eyes need Vitamin A to stay healthy. Good sources of this vitamin include

   ________________________ and ________________________.

2. Our teeth and gums need Vitamin C and Vitamin A to stay healthy. One food with both of these vitamins is ________________________.

3. When we get a cut, Vitamin C helps it stop bleeding. Some foods with Vitamin C are

   ________________________ and ________________________.

4. Vitamin E helps our bodies fight germs and disease. We can find Vitamin E in foods such as

   ________________________ and ________________________.

5. Even our skin benefits from vitamins! Vitamins ______________ and ______________

   help our skin stay healthy.

6. Vitamins A and E, as well as iron, help our body make red blood cells. Red blood cells carry oxygen through our bodies. Two foods that have iron are ________________________ and

   ________________________.

7. Five vitamins in the B-vitamin group help our heart stay healthy. Good sources of these vitamins are ________________________ and ________________________.

8. Vitamins C and K help us build strong bones. Vitamin C is found in foods such as

   ________________________ and ________________________.

   We get Vitamin K from ________________________ and ________________________.

9. Vitamin E helps keep our muscles strong and healthy. Some foods with Vitamin E are

   ______________________, ______________________, and ______________________,

10. We get Vitamin B and iron from foods such as ________________________ and

    ________________________.

Name

Vitamins and Minerals

Directions: Refer to the Vitamins and Minerals Chart on page 49 to help answer the questions.

1. Which fruits are good sources of calcium? ____________________

   ____

2. Name a vitamin we get from yogurt. ____________________

3. Which nutrients help our blood clot so we stop bleeding when we get a cut or larger wound?

   ____

4. How do B-vitamins help us? ____________________

   ____

5. It is important to eat orange fruits and vegetables such as apricots, carrots, and sweet potatoes. These foods are good sources of vitamin __________ which helps us

   ____________________.

6. Explain how vitamin C helps us. ____________________

   ____

7. What is an important nutrient we get from bananas? ____________________

   What does it do for us? ____________________

   ____

8. Why is it good to eat leafy green vegetables? ____________________

   ____

9. We eat Vitamin D from eggs, fish, and milk. Vitamin D helps us ____________________

   ____________________.

10. Why are dried beans and peas healthy foods to eat? ____________________

    ____

Name

Calories Equal Energy

Foods in the five food groups have nutrients that keep us healthy in many ways. Foods also have carbohydrates, fats, and protein. These things provide energy. The right amount of healthy food each day provides us with the right amount of energy.

A *calorie* is a measure of energy. Different foods have different amounts of calories. The number of calories each person needs varies. Some people need about twelve hundred calories per day. Others need over two thousand calories per day. Athletes can consume even more. It depends on a person's age, gender, and how active he or she is. Your calories (energy from food) should be *balanced* between these three areas:

Protein found in foods such as meat, fish, chicken, eggs, and milk

Carbohydrates found in foods such as whole grains, milk, fruits, vegetables

Healthy Fats found in foods such as avocados, olives, nuts, seeds, fish

Directions: List healthy foods you eat that go in each section.

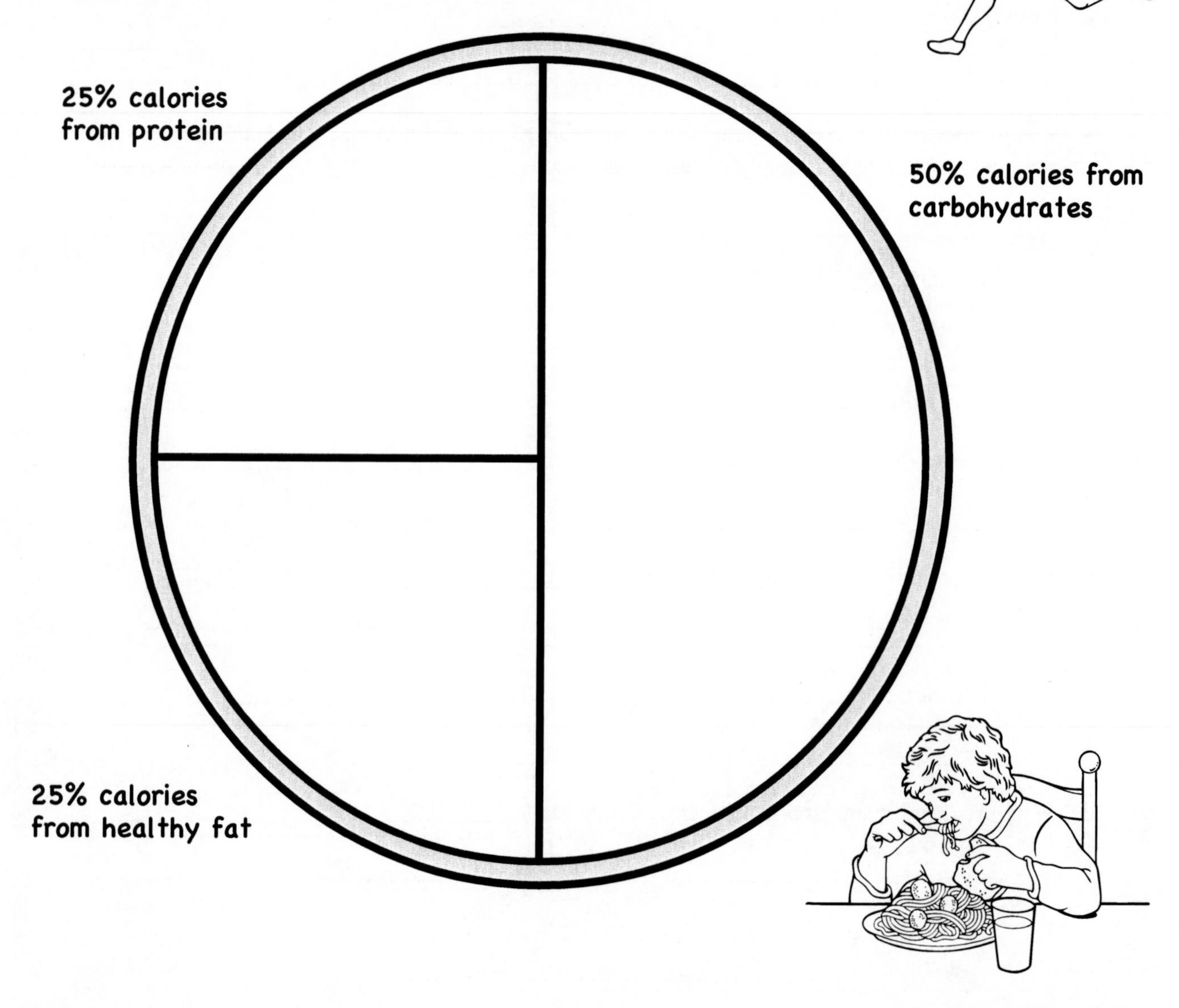

Name

What Is Junk Food?

It is important to check the ingredients in the foods you choose to eat. There are healthy foods, and there are foods we sometimes call "junk foods." We call them junk foods because they have higher levels of calories from sugar or fat but do not provide much protein, vitamins, or minerals. They are not as good for us. It is suggested that we eat junk foods for special treats and to watch portion sizes.

For example, let's look at french fries. Most of us enjoy eating french fries. But it is important to know what you are eating and how much! Look at the three different options for french fries below. First, look at the difference in serving sizes between the small and supersized french fries. It is quite a bit, isn't it? Then, look at the fat calories and the amounts of sodium. Which size order of fries might be healthier for you? Finally, look at the baked sweet potato fries. Compare them to the regular fries. What did you find?

Small French Fries

Nutrition Facts
Serving Size 1 serving (68g)
Servings Per Container 1

Amount Per Serving	%Daily Value*
Calories 210 — Calories from Fat 90	
Total Fat 10g	15 %
Saturated Fat 1.5g	8 %
Trans Fat 0g	
Cholesterol 0mg	0 %
Sodium 135mg	6 %
Total Carbohydrate 26g	9 %
Dietary Fiber 2g	8 %
Sugars 0g	
Protein 3g	
Vitamin A 0% • Vitamin C 15%	
Calcium 0% • Iron 2%	

* Percent Daily Values are based on a 2,000 calorie diet.

LOW=5% or less HIGH=20% or more

Supersized French Fries

Nutrition Facts
Serving Size 1 serving (176g)
Servings Per Container 1

Amount Per Serving	%Daily Value*
Calories 540 — Calories from Fat 230	
Total Fat 26g	40 %
Saturated Fat 4.5g	23 %
Trans Fat 0g	
Cholesterol 0mg	0 %
Sodium 350mg	15 %
Total Carbohydrate 68g	23 %
Dietary Fiber 6g	24 %
Sugars 0g	
Protein 8g	
Vitamin A 0% • Vitamin C 35%	
Calcium 2% • Iron 8%	

* Percent Daily Values are based on a 2,000 calorie diet.

LOW=5% or less HIGH=20% or more

Baked Sweet Potato Fries

Nutrition Facts
Serving Size 93.5g

Amount Per Serving	% Daily Value*
Calories 103 — Calories from Fat 22	
Total Fat 2.4g	4%
Saturated Fat 0.3g	2%
Trans Fat 0.0g	
Cholesterol 0mg	0%
Sodium 324mg	13%
Total Carbohydrates 18.8g	6%
Dietary Fiber 3.0g	12%
Sugars 5.8g	
Protein 1.8g	
Vitamin A 348% • Vitamin C 30%	
Calcium 4% • Iron 4%	

* Based on a 2000 calorie diet

Nutritional details are an estimate and should only be used as a guide for approximation.

caloriecount.about.com

Name a "junk food" you like. How could it be made a healthy food or what might be substituted for it?

____

____

Journal Page: Practice healthy eating for a week. Then pick a day and try to eat only healthy foods. Log them into your journal on the "My Healthy Foods Day" page.

Name

What Is Fiber?

Fiber comes from plants. It is the part of the plant that our bodies cannot break down to use for energy. There are two types of fiber:

Type 1—The first type of fiber dissolves in water. This type of fiber helps keep our blood sugar at the right level. (It also lowers cholesterol.) We can find this type of fiber in many foods. Whole grains such as barley and oatmeal have this kind of fiber. We find it in fruits such as apples, blueberries, oranges, pears, plums, and strawberries. Protein foods such as lentils, nuts, flaxseeds, and beans have this type of fiber. Some vegetables have it, too, such as cucumbers, celery, and carrots.

Type 2—The second type of fiber does not dissolve in water. This type helps us digest our food. High-fiber foods often have many nutrients and are low-calorie foods. Whole grain foods are good sources of this type of fiber. Vegetables such as celery, broccoli, cabbage, and carrots have this type of fiber. We also find it in dark leafy vegetables, raisins, and grapes.

Directions: Read the three nutrition labels below and answer the questions.

1. Which food has the most grams of fiber? ______________________________
2. Which food has the most vitamin C? ______________________________
3. What is one other nutrition fact you learned from reading the labels? ______________________________

____

Apple

Nutrition Facts	
Serving Size 1 apple (138g)	
Servings Per Container 10	
Amount Per Serving	
Calories 80	
	%Daily Value*
Total Fat 0g	0 %
Saturated Fat 0g	0 %
Trans Fat 0g	
Cholesterol 0mg	0 %
Sodium 0mg	0 %
Total Carbohydrate 21g	7 %
Dietary Fiber 4g	15 %
Sugars 18g	
Protein 0g	
Vitamin A 0% • Vitamin C 15%	
Calcium 0% • Iron 0%	
* Percent Daily Values are based on a 2,000 calorie diet.	

LOW=5% or less HIGH=20% or more

Bread, Whole Wheat

Nutrition Facts	
Serving Size 1 slice (50g)	
Servings Per Container 15	
Amount Per Serving	
Calories 140 Calories from Fat 30	
	%Daily Value*
Total Fat 3g	5 %
Saturated Fat 0.5g	3 %
Trans Fat 0g	
Cholesterol 0mg	0 %
Sodium 340mg	14 %
Total Carbohydrate 24g	8 %
Dietary Fiber 3g	14 %
Sugars 0g	
Protein 4g	
Vitamin A 0% • Vitamin C 0%	
Calcium 2% • Iron 8%	
* Percent Daily Values are based on a 2,000 calorie diet.	

LOW=5% or less HIGH=20% or more

Potato, Baked

Nutrition Facts	
Serving Size 1 potato (202g)	
Servings Per Container 1	
Amount Per Serving	
Calories 220	
	%Daily Value*
Total Fat 0g	0 %
Saturated Fat 0g	0 %
Trans Fat 0g	
Cholesterol 0mg	0 %
Sodium 15mg	1 %
Total Carbohydrate 51g	17 %
Dietary Fiber 5g	19 %
Sugars 3g	
Protein 5g	
Vitamin A 0% • Vitamin C 45%	
Calcium 2% • Iron 15%	
* Percent Daily Values are based on a 2,000 calorie diet.	

LOW=5% or less HIGH=20% or more

Name

What Is Cholesterol?

Cholesterol is a type of fat. The right amount helps our organs work the way they should. Our livers make cholesterol for our bodies. We can get cholesterol from some foods, too, including meat, fish, eggs, butter, cheese, and milk. There are two types of cholesterol, **LDL** and **HDL**:

LDL carries cholesterol away from the liver into the body. We say LDL is the "bad cholesterol" because it can stick to blood vessels. This can cause heart disease or a stroke in the brain. Some fats in foods raise cholesterol levels in your blood. These types of fats are saturated and trans fats.

HDL is the other type of cholesterol. HDL carries cholesterol back to the liver. The liver breaks down the "bad" cholesterol. Exercise helps your body use good cholesterol. Some cholesterol can help us digest our food. Keeping a healthy weight can also help improve levels of "good" HDL in your blood.

- Low cholesterol foods are often low in fat. These are healthy foods such as fruits, vegetables, and whole grains. These foods are good for most people.
- What does it mean when someone has "high cholesterol?" It means their bodies make too much cholesterol. When too much cholesterol sticks to the inside of the blood vessels it can cause heart disease. This makes it hard for blood to flow to parts of the body. The heart has to work harder. People with high cholesterol need to be careful about how much fat they eat. Exercise and eating lower cholesterol foods like fruits, vegetables, and whole grains can help.

1. Write facts you have learned about good and bad cholesterol on the chart below.

HDL "Good" Cholesterol	
LDL "Bad" Cholesterol	

2. What is one way you can help your heart stay healthy? ______________________

____

Challenge: Find three foods that are low in cholesterol.

______________ ______________ ______________

Name

Sodium

Many foods have sodium in them. Sodium is the chemical name for salt. Our bodies need salt in small amounts. Small amounts of salt keep body fluids in balance. Salt helps our nerves, our muscles, and our heart work the way they should. However, too much salt can be unhealthy. People who eat too much salt can have a greater risk for heart disease.

How much salt do you need? It's easy to get more sodium than we need in one day.

- Eight-year-olds should have 1,000 mg of sodium each day.
- Nine- and ten-year-olds should have no more than 1,500 mg of sodium each day.

Read the nutrition label to find out how much sodium (salt) is in the food products you eat.

Try to choose foods that are lower in sodium. You can also lower your salt intake by not putting salt on food at the table.

The sample label on the right shows you where to find the sodium listed in a food. Sodium is highlighted for you with a gray bar.

Bagel

Nutrition Facts
Serving Size 1 bagel (71g)
Servings Per Container 5

Amount Per Serving	
Calories 200	Calories from Fat 10
	%Daily Value*
Total Fat 1g	2 %
Saturated Fat 0g	0 %
Trans Fat 0g	
Cholesterol 0mg	0 %
Sodium 380mg	16 %
Total Carbohydrate 38g	13 %
Dietary Fiber 2g	7 %
Sugars 2g	
Protein 7g	
Vitamin A 0%	Vitamin C 0%
Calcium 6%	Iron 15%

* Percent Daily Values are based on a 2,000 calorie diet.

Directions: Collect nutrition labels from three foods. Look at the labels and find how much sodium is in each food. How much sodium is in each of the three foods you researched?

Food 1— ______________________ **Amount of Sodium** ____________

Food 2— ______________________ **Amount of Sodium** ____________

Food 3— ______________________ **Amount of Sodium** ____________

Add your three sodium (salt) totals. How much sodium did you get altogether from the three foods?

Food 1— ____________

Food 2— ____________

+ Food 3— ____________

____

Total ____________ **mg**

Did you go over 1,500mg? **Yes** **No**

What could you do to lower the amount of salt in your diet? ______________________

____

Name

Sugar

Do you know how much sugar is in the foods you eat? You can often find out by checking the nutrition label. Sometimes sugar is a natural part of a food, like the sugar in an apple. Other food items, like cookies or sweetened drinks, have sugar added. The label on the right shows you where to find the amount of sugar in a food. This label is for a medium-sized apple. The bottom label is for a cola drink.

The amounts of nutrients listed on labels are for *one serving* of that food. Sometimes people eat more than one serving of a food at a time. For example, the label might list one serving of cereal as one-half cup. If you have one cup of cereal for breakfast, you are having two servings of that food. That means you will have double the calories and other nutrients.

Directions: Check the labels to find the amounts of sugar in three things you eat in one day. If possible, bring labels from the empty food containers or the wrappers to class. Compare them with labels your classmates bring.

List the three food items you brought or checked. Read the nutrition label to see how much sugar was in each item. List the amount of sugar for each food.

Apple

Nutrition Facts
Serving Size 1 medium 3" dia 182g (182 g)

Amount Per Serving	
Calories 95	Calories from Fat 3
	% Daily Value*
Total Fat 0g	0%
Saturated Fat 0g	0%
Trans Fat	
Cholesterol 0mg	0%
Sodium 2mg	0%
Total Carbohydrate 25g	8%
Dietary Fiber 4g	17%
Sugars 19g	
Protein 0g	
Vitamin A 2% • Vitamin C	14%
Calcium 1% • Iron	1%

*Percent Daily Values are based on a 2,000 calorie diet. Your daily values may be higher or lower depending on your calorie needs:

	Calories	2,000	2,500
Total Fat	Less than	65g	80g
Sat Fat	Less than	20g	25g
Cholesterol	Less than	300mg	300mg
Sodium	Less than	2,400mg	2,400mg
Total Carbohydrate		300g	375g
Fiber		25g	30g

Calories per gram:
Fat 9 • Carbohydrate 4 • Protein 4

Food 1— ______________ **Amount of Sugar** ______________

Food 2— ______________ **Amount of Sugar** ______________

Food 3— ______________ **Amount of Sugar** ______________

Cola

Nutrition Facts
Serving Size 8 fl oz (240g)
Servings Per Container 1.5

Amount Per Serving	
Calories 100	
	%Daily Value*
Total Fat 0g	0 %
Saturated Fat 0g	0 %
Trans Fat 0g	
Cholesterol 0mg	0 %
Sodium 35mg	0 %
Total Carbohydrate 27g	9 %
Dietary Fiber 0g	0 %
Sugars 27g	
Protein 0g	
Vitamin A 0% •	Vitamin C 0%
Calcium 0% •	Iron 0%

* Percent Daily Values are based on a 2,000 calorie diet.

One teaspoon of sugar = 4 grams

It is important to try not to have more than 24 grams of added sugar per day. Add your three sugar totals.

How much sugar did you get from the three foods altogether?

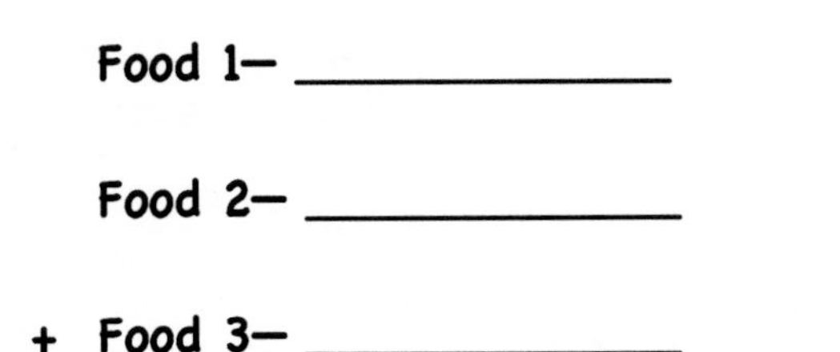

Food 1— ______________

Food 2— ______________

+ Food 3— ______________

____

Total ______________ **grams**

Teacher Note: The USDA provides a series of Nutrition Fact Cards like the ones featured in this book. They are downloadable and wonderful resources for comparing nutrition labels. See page 5 for the website address.

Name

Added Sugar

It is better if we eat healthy foods every day and save treats for special times. We know that foods like cookies, candy, ice cream, and some drinks have *added* sugar. It is easy to check the nutrition labels to see how much sugar is in the packaged foods you eat.

Bananas and oranges have quite a bit of natural sugar. Tomatoes and snow peas have a little natural sugar. These are still healthy foods because they have many other nutrients. Milk also has sugar in it, but it is not added sugar.

Some health organizations say children should have no more than six teaspoons of *added* sugar per day. This is sugar that has been added to the food and is not there naturally.

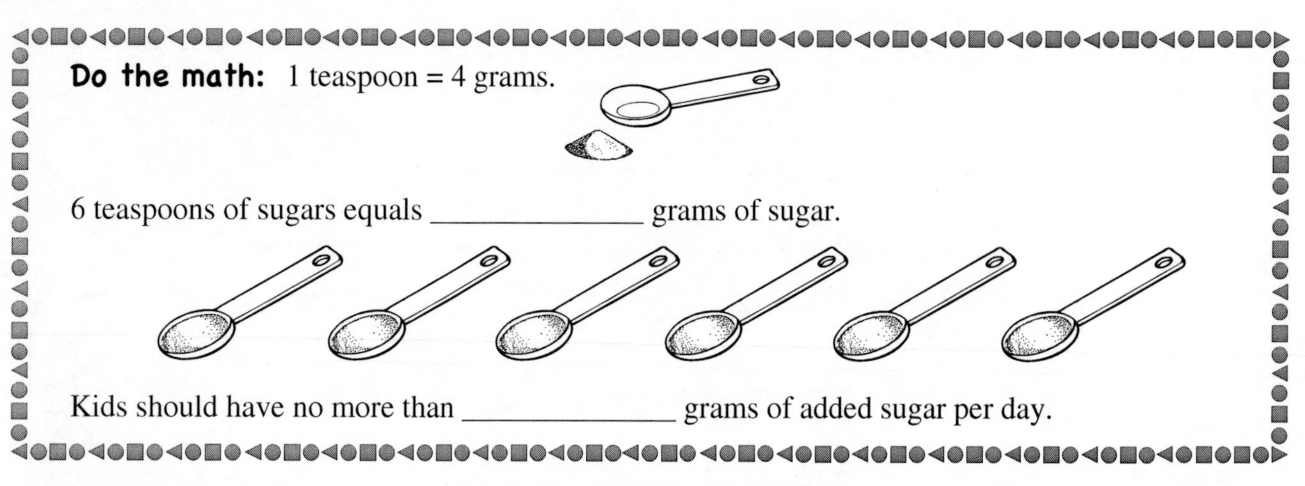

Do the math: 1 teaspoon = 4 grams.

6 teaspoons of sugars equals _____________ grams of sugar.

Kids should have no more than _____________ grams of added sugar per day.

Directions: Read the chart below that shows how much hidden sugar is in everyday foods. Do the math to fill in the missing spaces on the chart. Round your answers as needed to find an estimate.

Food	Grams of Sugar per Serving	Teaspoons
barbecue sauce	13 g	
graham crackers	7 g	
granola bars		2 teaspoons (average)
peanut butter	3 g	
raisin bran cereal		4 teaspoons (average)
saltine crackers		0 teaspoons
spaghetti sauce	8 g (average)	
yogurt		6 teaspoons

1. Which food surprised you most with its amount of sugar? ____________________________

2. Which two foods have the same amount of sugar per serving?

____________________________ ____________________________

Name

Why Water?

Did you know that human beings can live up to 40 days without food but only seven days without water? It is true! Water is so important that most of our body is made up of it. Almost three quarters of our total body weight is water. This includes water in our tissues, our blood, and our bones. Our bodies use water every day, and that water needs to be replaced. We get most of the water we need from the foods we eat. Most foods are almost half water, but we also need to drink liquids. Drinking water makes the most sense, and most people should drink more water than they do.

Our bodies need water to live. We need to supply our bodies with water every day. Water . . .

- transports the nutrients from the foods we eat to different parts of our bodies.
- helps us digest our food.
- carries wastes out of the body.
- helps keep our bodies cool.
- helps chemicals in our bodies react properly with one another.
- keeps our eyes moist and helps our joints move—it lubricates.
- may help reduce a fever.
- can reduce swelling or pain from bruises.
- helps people relax and eases pain in sore muscles.
- can help clean and heal burns.
- helps us feel full, which helps us eat the right amounts of food instead of eating too much.

1. Young people should have about eight cups of liquid each day. (1 cup = 8 oz.) Look at the 8 oz. glasses below. If about one quarter of our water comes from the foods we eat, how much more water do we need to drink? Shade the glasses to show the amount.

2. You need extra water when you exercise and play sports. You need at least one half cup for every 20 minutes you play. How much extra water should you drink if you are going to play soccer for an hour? Shade the glasses to show the amount.

3. What are two ways drinking water helps you?

   a. ____

   b. ____

Challenge: Work with a partner to create a poster describing the health benefits of drinking water.

Journal Page: Complete the "Let's Talk About Water" journal page on page 87.

Name

Food Tips for Tip-Top Health

Are you in tip-top health? Which of the following tips do you think you follow best? Which ones do you feel you have to improve? What steps can you take to eat healthier?

Food Tips

1. Read nutrition labels. Check serving sizes and the amount of healthy nutrients in each serving.
2. Enjoy your food without overeating. Portion your food on a plate according to the USDA recommended guidelines.
3. Throughout the day, eat foods from each group. Choose food products that are lower in sugar, fat, and sodium content.
4. Focus on fruits and vegetables by filling about half your plate with them.
5. Drink water instead of sugary soft drinks and juices.
6. Balance good eating habits with daily physical activity and enough sleep.

Directions: Choose one tip and write a short paragraph explaining how you can improve your eating habits by following that tip.

Name

How Much Is a Serving?

A serving is the suggested amount of food to eat at a meal or for a snack. Eating the right amount helps us stay at a healthy weight. We should eat a variety of foods but not too much of any one kind. The variety helps us get all the nutrients we need. A guide for how much of a food is enough is right in our hands! Keep these hints in mind when you are trying to figure out the right amount to eat at a meal:

- Make your hand into a fist. One serving, or portion, of rice, pasta, fruit, vegetables, or yogurt is roughly the size of your fist.
- A serving of cheese is about the size of your thumb. Can you believe it?
- A serving of most snack foods is a handful.
- A serving of meat or fish will fit in your palm.

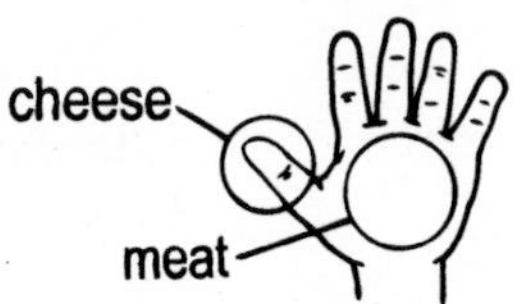

Another way to do this is to think about common objects when choosing amounts to eat in a serving:

- $\frac{1}{4}$ cup (1/4 c.) serving is the size of a large egg.
- $\frac{1}{2}$ cup (1/2 c.) serving is the size of half a baseball.
- 1 cup (1 c.) serving is the same as an adult fist or a whole baseball.

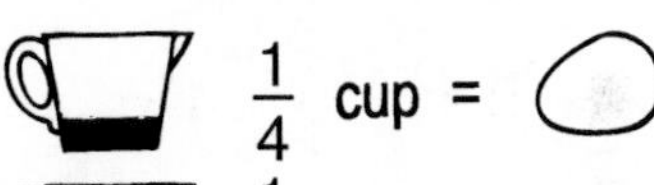
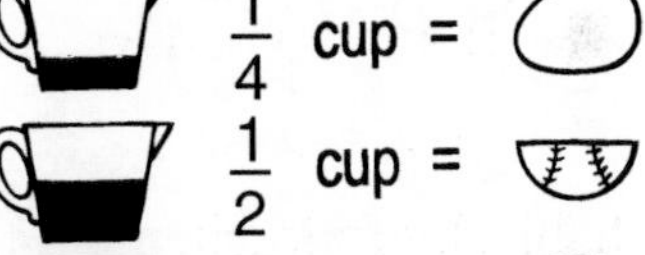

Directions: Look at the serving suggestions. Think about the foods you might eat to meet those suggestions. Then, fill in the menu on page 62.

Fruit

3 servings each day

How much is a serving?
- 1 med. fruit
- $\frac{1}{2}$ cup chopped, cooked, or canned fruit
- $\frac{3}{4}$ c. juice

Vegetables

4 servings each day

How much is a serving?
- 1 c. leafy greens
- $\frac{1}{2}$ c. cooked or raw vegetables
- $\frac{3}{4}$ c. juice

Dairy

3 servings each day

How much is a serving?
- 1 cup milk or yogurt
- $1\frac{1}{2}$ oz. cheese

Grains

5 servings each day; half should be whole grains

How much is a serving?
- 1 slice bread
- $\frac{1}{2}$ c. cooked rice, pasta, or cereal
- 1 c. ready-to-eat cereal
- 5 whole-wheat crackers
- 3 cups popped popcorn

Meat/Protein

5 servings each day

How much is a serving?
- $\frac{1}{2}$ c. cooked dry beans
- 3 oz. cooked meat or palm size
- 1 large egg
- 2 tablespoons peanut butter = 1 oz.
- $\frac{1}{4}$ c. nuts = 1 oz.

Name

Plan a Menu

Directions: Create a menu plan for one day. Try to balance the right number of servings of each food group. Use the serving suggestions on page 61 for a reference. Later, evaluate your choices and think about changes you could make.

Breakfast

Snack:

Lunch

Snack:

Dinner

Journal Page: Pick a day and try to eat only healthy foods. Log these foods into your journal on the "My Healthy Foods Day" page.

Name

So Many Healthy Foods!

Directions: Read the clues on each card to find the correct answer. Do research if needed.

1. This whole grain is used to make bread.

This whole grain is used to make tortillas.

The grain is also called a vegetable.

We get fiber, protein, and iron from this food. ____________________

2. This dairy food is similar to a food made in Europe.

Sometimes it has holes in it.

It makes a good snack food.

This food is a good source of protein and calcium. ____________________

3. Many people like to snack on this protein food.

We eat the kernels from the flower.

The seeds are also pressed to make oil.

This food also gives us fiber. ____________________

4. This fruit has fuzzy brown skin. It is green on the inside.

Some people think it tastes like a cross between a strawberry and a banana.

You can scoop it out of its skin with a spoon or peel it and slice it to eat.

This fruit is a great source of vitamin C. ____________________

5. This is a stone fruit.

We eat it like a vegetable or make a dip with it.

Some people call it an "alligator pear" because of its appearance.

This food is a good source of fiber and vitamin C. ____________________

6. This green vegetable is good with a dip.

Some people eat it with peanut butter.

The part of the plant we eat is the stem.

This low-calorie snack gives us fiber and vitamin A. ____________________

Name

Food Safety

Eating healthy food helps us grow and stay well. Sometimes, though, people do get sick from the food they eat. It is important to keep our food safe. If we handle food safely, we'll get the healthy benefits from the foods we eat. If not, we might get sick. Read the food safety rules below:

- Wash your hands in warm, soapy water to remove germs before you touch food.
- Cover your mouth and nose when you sneeze. Turn your head away from the food, too. Then wash your hands.
- Wash fruits and vegetables before cutting or preparing them.
- Wash the cutting board with a disinfectant after each use to prevent germs from spreading to other foods.
- Keep hot foods hot. Use the refrigerator to keep cold foods cold.
- Keep raw meat away from other foods. Try to use a different cutting board for fruits and vegetables.

1. What's wrong with the picture? ____

____

____

2. Why is it important to follow safety rules when you are storing or preparing food?

____

____

____

____

3. Discuss your answers with a partner. What else did you learn? ______________

____

____

____

Name

Healthy Lifestyles

1. Listen as a teacher or selected students read the healthy lifestyles statements below. After each statement, follow one of the movement directions in the box.

- Raise your arms straight up if this is something you do all the time.
- Put your hands on your head if you do this some of the time.
- Hold your arms straight out in front of you if you are just getting started doing this in your life.

2. Fill in the box next to any statement you already do all the time.

- ☐ I try to watch my portions and eat just the right amount of food.
- ☐ I eat plenty of fruits and vegetables each day.
- ☐ I do not share drinks with others.
- ☐ I choose to drink water, especially between meals.
- ☐ I exercise every day.
- ☐ I wash my hands before I eat.
- ☐ I try to make healthy choices when eating away from home.
- ☐ I eat a healthy breakfast every day.
- ☐ I cover my mouth when I cough or sneeze.
- ☐ I get plenty of sleep each day.
- ☐ I take care of my teeth each day.
- ☐ I watch how many "sometimes" foods I eat each week.
- ☐ I follow safety rules on the playground and when playing sports.

Just the right amount.

No, I already had a treat today.

3. Which healthy habit will you work on next? How?______________________________

____

Name

Make a "Healthy Me" Mini-Book

Directions: Write a "mini-book" story about a day in your life when you are practicing a healthy lifestyle. Plan to include pictures with your story. Remember what you have learned about eating healthy foods. Think about other things people do to stay healthy, such as exercising, germ prevention, and getting enough rest. You might write about what you and your friends do to stay healthy.

1. Use scratch paper or the back of this page to plan your story. It will have a cover and seven "book" pages.
2. Follow the directions below to create the mini book. Use a white sheet of paper. (If possible, use 11" × 17" paper to allow more room for illustrations.)
3. Create a title page.
4. Copy your 7-page story into the book and illustrate it.

How to Make a Mini-Book

Step 1: Hold the paper tall (short-side at top). Fold down, then across, then down again. You should now have 8 rectangular sections.

Step 2: Open the paper to the first fold. Cut halfway down. This will create the slit.

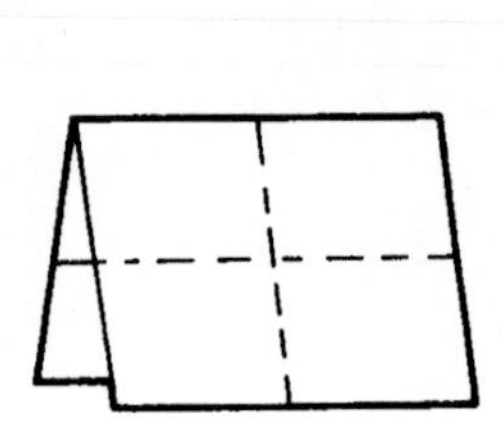

Step 3: Open the paper so the slit is now on the top. You should have a long strip with four boxes.

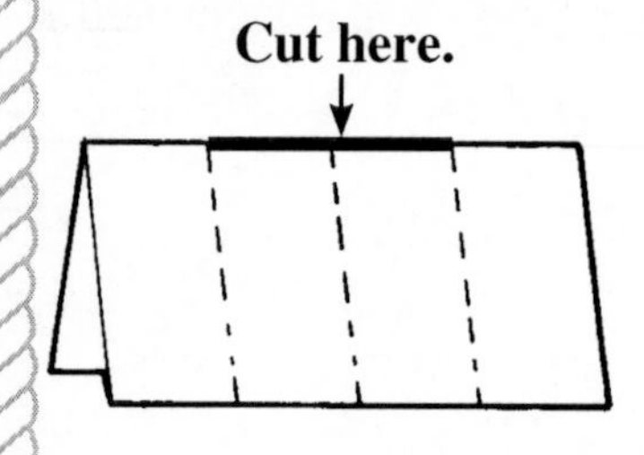

Step 4: Push the two edges together so the cut pages form a square.

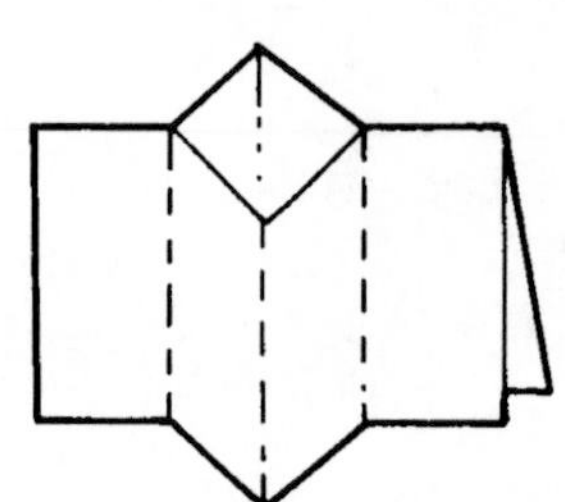

Step 5: Continue pushing until the square is gone.

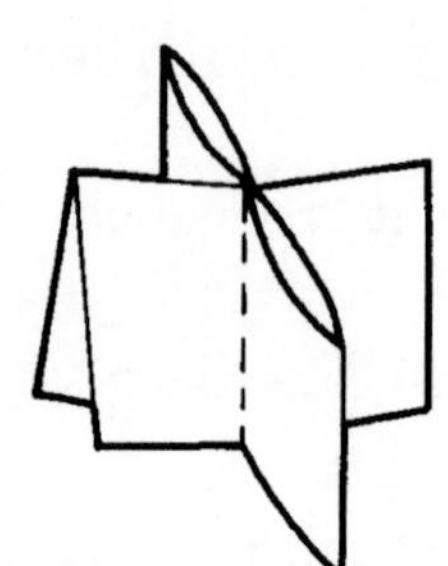

Step 6: Fold all the pages and crease them. You should have an 8-page book.

Name

Dental Health

Eating healthy foods helps our teeth and gums stay healthy. We also keep our teeth healthy by brushing and flossing after eating. Flossing our teeth removes the bits of food that get stuck where a toothbrush cannot reach.

Our teeth need calcium and the other nutrients we get from our food to grow strong and healthy. We need our teeth to help us chew our foods so we can digest them.

Types of Teeth

Our front teeth are called **incisors**. They cut food and guide it into our mouths. Next to our four front teeth are the **cuspids**. Some people call them **canine** teeth because they have one point. They help us tear foods such as vegetables and meat. **Bicuspids** are right behind the cuspids. They replace your first and second **molars** when you are between about nine and eleven years old. They have larger flat surfaces to chew and grind food into smaller bits for swallowing.

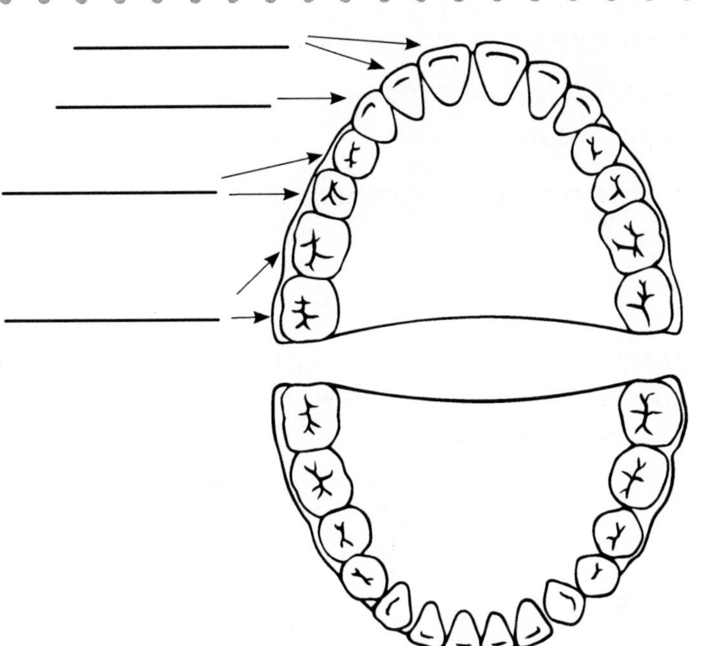

1. Label the types of teeth.

Parts of a Tooth

Each tooth has a crown and a root. The **crown** sits above the gum line and is the part of the tooth we see when we open our mouth. The **root** of the tooth is below the gum line.

The white part that covers the tooth is called the **enamel**. It protects our teeth when we bite and chew food. **Dentin** forms most of the tooth and supports the enamel. It is a little like bone and has some nerves that tell us if something is wrong with a tooth. The **pulp** is soft tissue inside the tooth. It contains blood vessels and nerves. It nourishes the tooth and sends signals to the brain.

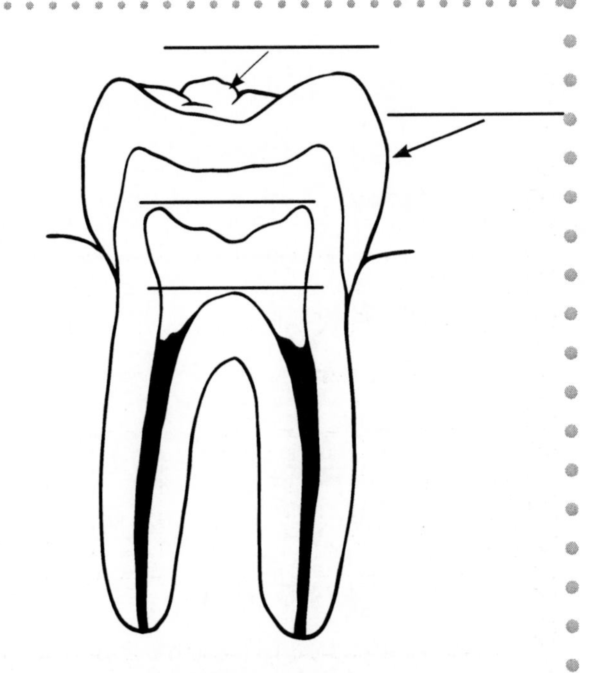

2. Label the parts of a tooth.

Name

Get Enough Sleep

Light helps us wake up in the morning. When it gets dark, our bodies get sleepy. This is a natural sleep cycle. Sleep helps our muscles, bones, and skin grow and repair injuries. Sleep helps our brains rest, too. When we are rested, we are more alert and more able to learn. How much sleep is enough? Young people need 10 to 11 hours of sleep each night.

Our bodies need rest to have energy each day. When we are rested. . .

- we have the energy we need.
- we can concentrate better, solve problems, and think of new ideas.
- we don't get sick as often because our bodies are better able to fight off disease.
- we get along better with our friends and family.

Directions: Record your sleep hours and your level of energy each day this week. On Friday, review the data to see how healthy your sleep patterns are.

1. Fill in the number of hours of sleep you got the night before at the beginning of each school day.
2. Mark your energy level on the chart at the end of class each day. Circle the appropriate word in the box.

Night	Hours of Sleep	Energy Level
Monday		Low → Medium → High
Tuesday		Low → Medium → High
Wednesday		Low → Medium → High
Thursday		Low → Medium → High

3. Evaluate the chart on Friday. How was your energy level? ____________________
4. Do you get enough sleep? ____________________
5. What can you do to improve your sleep routine? ____________________

Name

Physical Safety

Staying safe is one way we stay healthy. There are things we can do to stay safe in our daily lives.

Directions: Work with a partner. Fill in each blank with a word that makes sense. Discuss answers.

Getting Around Town

1. The best place to cross the street is at a ______________________.
2. Check for oncoming ______________________ even if you have a walk signal.
3. Pay attention to parked ______________________ when crossing at an intersection.
4. Some barriers that might keep cars from seeing you include tall______________________, or ______________________.
5. Leave a ______________________ around you when you are riding your bike.
6. Wear a ______________________ when riding a bike, skateboard, or scooter.
7. Follow traffic safety ______________________ when riding a bike, skateboard, or scooter.

School Bus Safety

1. Talk ______________________ when riding the school bus.
2. Keep aisles ______________________ on the school bus.
3. Follow the driver's ______________________ rules about safety when riding the school bus.
4. Step far enough ______________________ from the bus so that the bus driver can see you before he or she moves on.
5. Wait for the bus driver's ______________________ before you cross the road.
6. Look both ways to make sure cars have stopped before ______________________ in front of the bus.

Stranger Danger

1. It is not a good idea to talk to a stranger or accept a ride or a gift from someone we do not ______________________.
2. Some people we do not know can ______________________ us, such as police officers or store security people.
3. You might be in a situation that is uncomfortable or seems dangerous. You should say ______________________ if the person asks you to do something or leave with him or her. ______________________ a trusted adult what happened.
4. Follow the safety ______________________ for your household about answering the door or the phone.
5. What are your home safety rules? Write them on the back of this page.

Name

Physical Fitness

What does *physical fitness* mean? When we are "physically fit," we feel good, we eat well, and we get enough sleep. This gives us enough energy to do the things we want to do each day. Being in good shape (fit) helps us stay at a healthy weight. It helps our bodies fight illnesses, too.

Physically fit people get exercise at least three days each week.

There are many factors to fitness:

- Running, jumping, walking distances, swimming, climbing, and cycling are forms of **aerobic exercise**. This type of exercise helps our bodies use oxygen well (breathing) and strengthens our hearts.
- **Muscle strength** is important, too. We can improve muscle strength by doing different exercises and running in short bursts (sprints) of a few seconds up to 2 minutes.

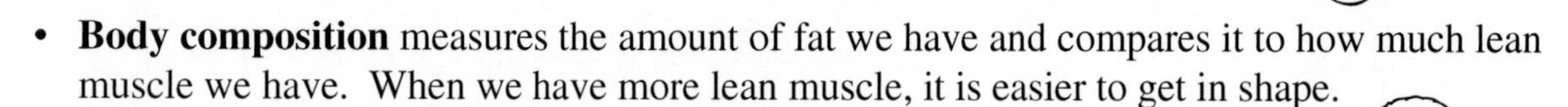

- **Body composition** measures the amount of fat we have and compares it to how much lean muscle we have. When we have more lean muscle, it is easier to get in shape.
- People who are fit tend to be more **agile** and **flexible**. This means they can move quickly and they can bend or change directions easily. One way to increase flexibility is to stretch. When we stretch we straighten different body parts to their full length. Always stretch gently and hold each stretch instead of bouncing.

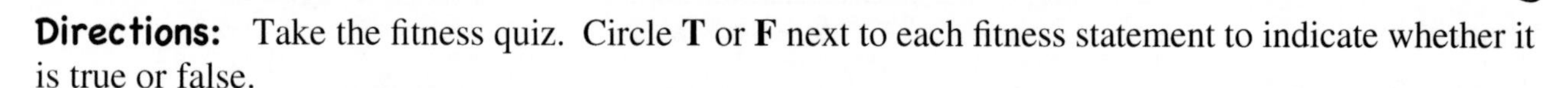

Directions: Take the fitness quiz. Circle **T** or **F** next to each fitness statement to indicate whether it is true or false.

Fitness Quiz		
T	F	**1.** Our bodies need exercise to breathe.
T	F	**2.** We should get aerobic exercise at least three times a week.
T	F	**3.** Our bodies should have more lean muscle than fat.
T	F	**4.** Sitting is an aerobic exercise.
T	F	**5.** We need to move our muscles to strengthen them.
T	F	**6.** Our muscles can never get any larger or stronger.
T	F	**7.** Stretching is a good way to maintain flexibility.
T	F	**8.** It is okay to bounce when stretching.
T	F	**9.** People who are agile cannot move or change direction quickly.
T	F	**10.** Being agile helps us stay safe.

Name

Heart Rate

Exercise helps our blood carry oxygen to all parts of our bodies. It also strengthens our heart muscles. Did you know your heart is a muscle?

To find your resting, or regular, heart rate, follow these steps:

1. Find your pulse on your wrist or neck.
2. Have someone watch a clock for 10 seconds while you count the beats of your heart.
3. Multiply by 6. The answer will be your resting heart rate for one minute.

Heart beats in 10 seconds: __________ X 6 = __________ beats per minute

You can check your heart rate to make sure you are exercising with enough effort to help your body. The rate that helps you benefit from exercise is called your **target heart rate**.

The target heart rate for 8–11-year-olds is around 130 beats per minute (bpm).

1. After you exercise, find your pulse on your wrist or neck.
2. Have someone watch a clock for 10 seconds while you count the beats of your heart.
3. Multiply by 6 to find your heart rate for one minute.

Heart beats in 10 seconds: __________ X 6 = __________ beats per minute

How close is your heart rate after exercise to your target heart rate?

Higher than 140 bpm ☐ **About 130 bpm** ☐ **Lower than 120 bpm** ☐

Directions: Use the chart below to track how your heart rate improves with regular exercise. The first line is an example.

Day	Exercise	Time	Heart Rate After Exercise
example	*running*	*20 minutes*	*150 bpm*
1.			
2.			
3.			
4.			
5.			
6.			
7.			

Name

Beanbags and Relays

Directions: Try the following activities for fun. They will help you stretch, focus on body movement, and improve your balance.

Beanbag Movement

Use small beanbags. Listen to any directions your teacher gives you. Try the following movements with the beanbag to get started. Place the beanbag. . .

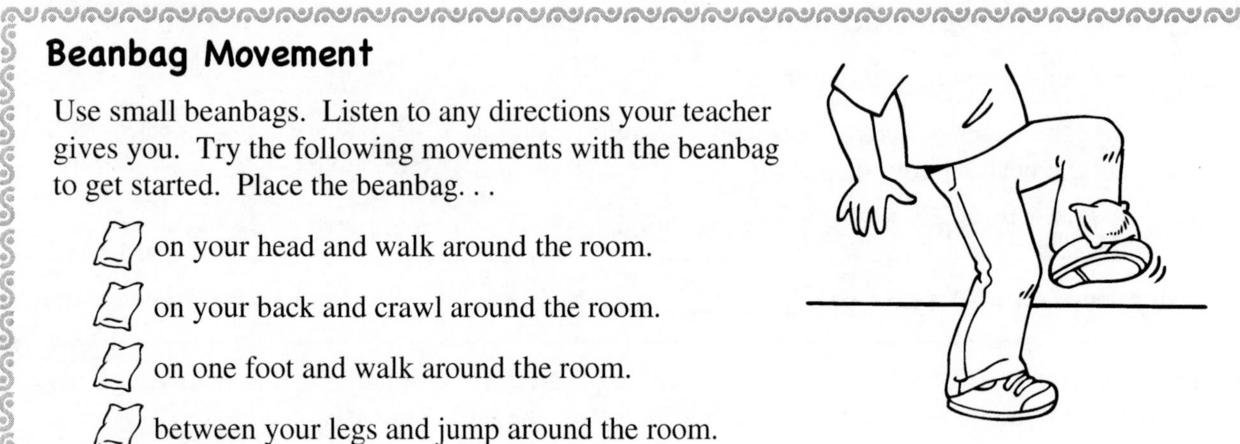

- on your head and walk around the room.
- on your back and crawl around the room.
- on one foot and walk around the room.
- between your legs and jump around the room.
- on your shoulder and walk backward around the room.

Beanbag Relay

1. Divide the class into teams. Each team will race against the others in a relay.
2. Walk to a determined point in the room (or outside). Listen as the teacher or other selected leader calls out movements for you to do. For example, the first time it is a student's turn, he or she will walk (from the predetermined point) with the beanbag on his or her head to another finishing point.
3. He or she will pass the beanbag to the next competitor on the team.
4. Once each student on the team has completed that activity, his or her beanbag should be placed on his or her foot.
5. The first team to have all of its members complete the action is the winner.

Name

Active Days

Directions: Use an action verb from the Word Box to describe each picture in a sentence.

1. ______________________________
2. ______________________________
3. ______________________________
4. ______________________________
5. ______________________________
6. ______________________________
7. ______________________________
8. ______________________________
9. ______________________________

Word Box			
	bouncing	skating	sliding
	crawling	skipping	stomping
	galloping	leaping	twisting

Challenge: Cut out the pictures and rank them from most active to least active.

Name

Machine Movements

A machine is a tool with more than one part. Machine parts move or work together to apply force to move objects. Machines can make many tasks easier for us.

1. Do some research about the different tools or machines. Then, match each one to a movement.

Movement	Machine
turns together	drill
grasps	pulley
moves up and down	crank and rod
turns and pushes	tongs
lifts	gears
rotates	wheels and axles
turns	lever

2. What are some ways you move like a machine every day?______________________________

____

____

____

Challenge: Work with a small group to design a machine. Determine which parts your machine will have and which person will move like each part. Demonstrate (act out) your machine for the class.

Name

Sports Field Day

We use many different movements and actions when we play sports. Think of the ways you move when you play your favorite sport.

Directions: Think about the sports below. Write action words for the movements used in the sport.

Challenge: Choose a sport to act out for the class. Use physical movements, not props. Try to guess which sports your classmates are demonstrating.

Name

Summer Fun

There are different kinds of camps to attend in the summer. Most camps have games and other activities.

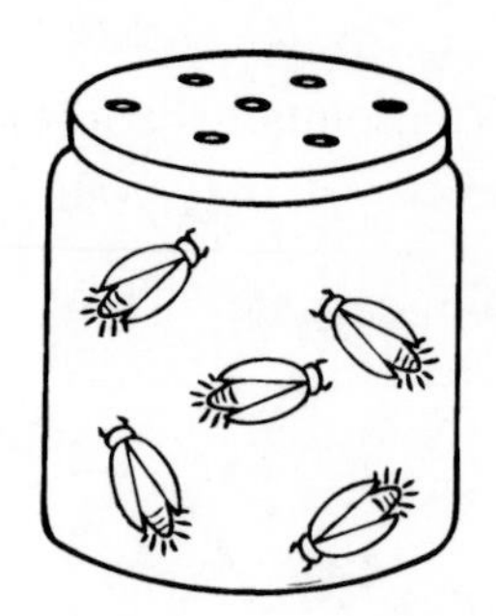

Directions: Pretend you are at summer camp. Practice the following activities with a partner. Focus on what skills are required and what muscles you would use.

- **reeling in a fish** ______________________________
- **catching fireflies in a jar** ______________________________
- **swimming** ______________________________
- **climbing a tree** ______________________________
- **shooting a basketball** ______________________________
- **playing volleyball** ______________________________
- **rowing a boat** ______________________________
- **hiking up a mountain** ______________________________
- **riding a horse** ______________________________

Name

Fitness Challenge

A **challenge** is a test of one's abilities. It might be something new that has not been practiced. It could require strength, agility, or a specific skill. Try each of the challenges below for one minute. See if you can improve the second or third time you try each activity.

Challenge	1st Time	2nd Time	3rd Time
1. How many times can you toss a beanbag and catch it?			
2. How many times can you clap your hands between tossing and catching a beanbag?			
3. How many seconds or minutes can you dribble a ball?			
4. How many times can you bounce a ball against the wall and catch it?			
5. How many times can you bat a balloon or ball in the air?			
6. How far can you skip on a line in 30 seconds?			
7. How far can you jump from a standing position?			
8. How long can you balance on your left foot?			
9. How long can you balance on your right foot?			
10. How many times can you hop back and forth in 30 seconds?			

★ **Challenge:** Think of a fitness challenge for your classmates to try. ______________________

____

Name

The World Around You

The world in which we live offers many opportunities to stay active and fit.

1. Read the list of ideas below. Check the box next to activities you could do.

   - ☐ Lift your schoolbooks over your head 10 times before you do your homework. When you need a break, lift the books again 10 times.
   - ☐ Walk or run around a track at a local school. See if a member of your family will join you.
   - ☐ Help carry groceries in the house. Carry the milk back and forth a few times. If there is only one jug (container), carry it back and forth two or three times with each hand.
   - ☐ Help put the groceries away. Use a pair of small cans for weights:
     - Can you hold one can out in front of you and lift it over your head? How many times in a minute?
     - Can you lift both cans at once? How many times can you lift both cans in a minute?
   - ☐ Help with chores. Dance to music while you sweep, vacuum, or make the bed.
   - ☐ Rake leaves into a pile. Then put all the leaves in bags or containers.
   - ☐ Think of different (safe!) ways to climb the stairs. Go up two stairs, then back down one. Climb two more stairs, then go back down one. Continue to the top of the stairs.
   - ☐ Help family members plan an outing you can all do together. Perhaps you can walk or ride bikes on a path in your community.

2. Brainstorm other ways you can stay active in your community or neighborhood.

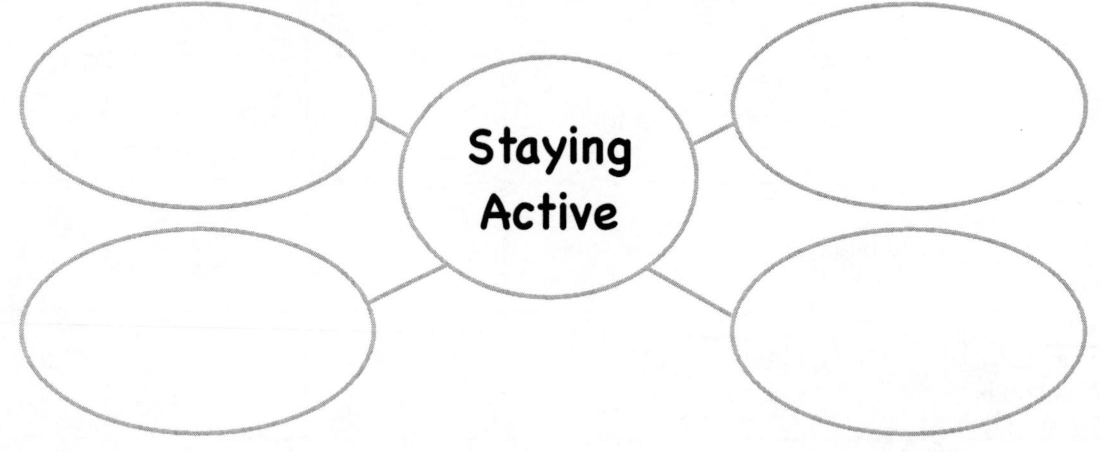

3. Set a goal of two things from the list or the web to try this week. Write your goals below.

   I will ____.

   I will____.

Name

Healthy Habits Game

Make a game about healthy habits to play with your friends.

1. Make a game board or enlarge the sample below. Include obstacles and shortcuts for players. (e.g., Hop ahead two spaces, you ate a salad! or Go back 3 spaces, you didn't exercise today!) Decorate it with pictures of healthy habits.
2. Create a set of 20 or more game cards. Number the cards. Each card should have a healthy habits question. Answers can be fill-in-the-blanks or True or False. Here are some suggestions:

Walking is good exercise.

True or **False**? ①

Broccoli is a healthy vegetable. We eat the stem and the flowers.

True or **False**? ②

Lemons, limes and ____________ are citrus fruits. ③

3. Create an answer key to match the numbers on the cards.
4. Play the game with your friends to review what you have learned. Each player will have a token, such as a button of a different color. Use a number cube, die, or a simple spinner to move around the game board.

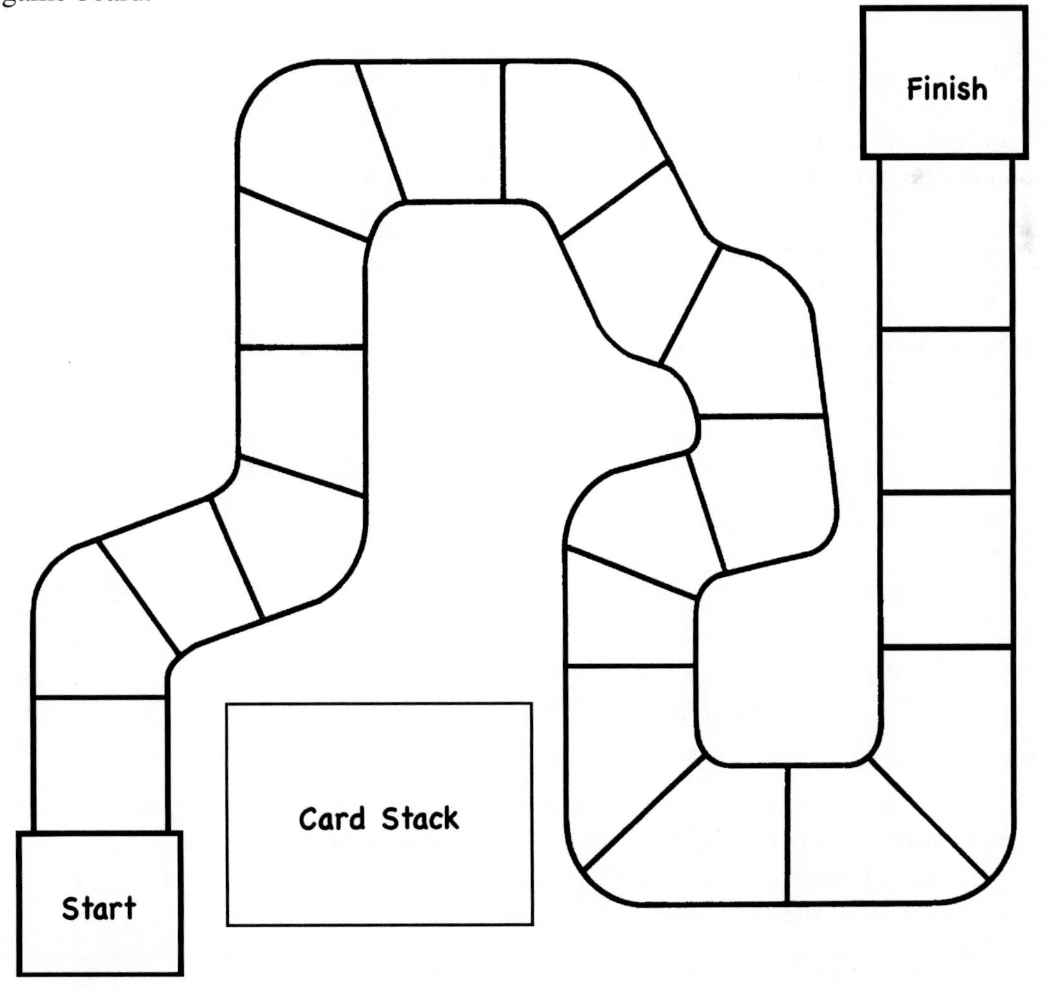

Name

Relay Activities

Relay 1

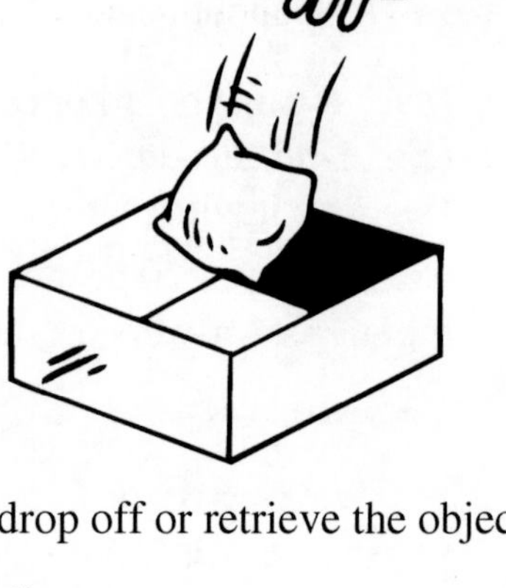

1. Set up the relay so that each team has an object with a target. You can use a box, can, or even a space marked on the floor with tape. Each team's object should fit in the target space.
2. The first team member will carry the object from the start to the finish, placing the object in the target before returning to the team.
3. The second player advances to retrieve the object from the target area and carries it back to the next team member.
4. Continue in this manner until all players have had an opportunity to drop off or retrieve the object.

Optional: Vary the ways students move from start to finish or vary the distances.

Relay 2

1. Divide students into teams (as many teams as balls and targets, such as baskets, available).
2. Have team members count off and remember their numbers!
3. Call a number at random, (e.g., number four). Each number four player will try to throw the ball in the target as many times as possible within a time set on a timer, (e.g., 10 or 20 seconds).

Relay 3

1. Set up the relay by writing different movements on cards or slips of paper. You will need a set of cards for each team.
2. Place each team's cards in a container at the start of the relay. Each player will draw a card from the container. The card will dictate the way in which he or she moves to get from the start to the finish.
3. Each subsequent player will draw a card from the container with a different movement.
4. Suggestions for movements include the following: *walk, walk backward, jog, jog backward, skip, hop, gallop, slide, jump, walk heel-to-toe, walk on tip-toe, walk on heels, crab walk, etc.*

Juggling

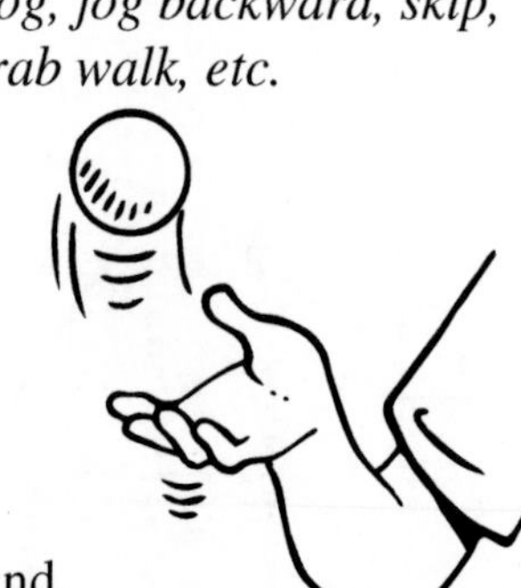

1. Have students try various juggling activities using scarves or small, lightweight balls.
2. Students should start with practicing tossing one scarf or ball and catching it with the same hand. Have them practice with each hand.
3. Students then progress to tossing two balls and catching one ball in each hand.

Teacher Note: Students may practice these moves with partners to make it easier. As students gain proficiency, they can try juggling three objects in a cascading circle, with one in the air as they are catching the other two.

Outdoor Activities

Capture the Flag

1. Invite students to try to capture an object, such as a cone, flag, or other piece of play equipment.
2. Place the object in the center of the playing space (or atop the cone), with students arranged around a marked perimeter.
3. Select a student to act as guard. Other players try to capture the object without getting caught.
4. If it is too easy for players to capture the object, the one who captures it must return to one of the corners of the marked area safely without being tagged.
5. Vary the game by using different objects, different names for the guard, and different ways to set up and capture.

Jumping Activities

Give students opportunities to develop coordination and endurance with these jumping activities (with or without jump ropes). Challenge students to try different steps and patterns when they jump.

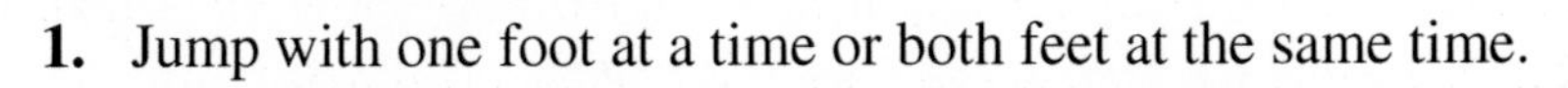

1. Jump with one foot at a time or both feet at the same time.
2. Have students spread their feet apart as they jump.
3. Mark a line on the ground with chalk. Have students stand with both feet on one side of the line. Then jump forward with both feet over the line. Have students try jumping forward and backward.
4. Challenge students to think of their own patterns of movement combining skips, hops, jumps, and different kinds of steps. Have students take turns sharing their patterns with the group. Arrange students in a circle or series of lines to follow the student leaders.

Food and Fitness JOURNAL

This journal belongs to:

Being Healthy

Being healthy is important. When you are healthy you can do many things. You can

To be healthy, you need to

Personal Health Goals

Directions: Write at least one personal health goal you would like to try each week. Check each week and see how you're doing at meeting your goal. Mark the date you meet each challenge.

	Met	Not Yet
WEEK ________________ My personal goal this week is to________________________________ ____		
WEEK ________________ My personal goal this week is to________________________________ ____		
WEEK ________________ My personal goal this week is to________________________________ ____		
WEEK ________________ My personal goal this week is to________________________________ ____		
WEEK ________________ My personal goal this week is to________________________________ ____		
WEEK ________________ My personal goal this week is to________________________________ ____		
WEEK ________________ My personal goal this week is to________________________________ ____		

My Most Important Foods

I have learned about the five food groups. Here is a food from each group that I eat and the reasons why I think it is healthy for me.

Fruit: ______________________________

It has the following nutrients:____

____

____

Vegetable: ______________________________

It has the following nutrients:____

____

____

Protein: ______________________________

It has the following nutrients:____

____

____

Dairy Product: ______________________________

It has the following nutrients:____

____

____

Grain Product: ______________________________

It has the following nutrients:____

____

____

I Didn't Know That!

I am learning more about healthy foods and healthy habits. Here are a few things I have learned this year and how I think I can use the information to be healthier.

Date: ______________________

I learned that ______________________

Now I know that ______________________

Date: ______________________

I learned that ______________________

Now I know that ______________________

Date: ______________________

I learned that ______________________

Now I know that ______________________

Date: ______________________

I learned that ______________________

Now I know that ______________________

Date: ______________________

I learned that ______________________

Now I know that______________________

The most useful thing I have learned about eating healthy foods and having healthy habits is

____

____

____

____

____

____

____

Let's Talk About Water

Water is important to me because...

My Healthy Foods Day

These are the healthy foods I ate today.

Breakfast

Snack:

Lunch

Snack:

Dinner

Junk Food

Junk food is not a healthy choice because…

I Am In Charge

Pretend it is your job to feed the students in your class lunch today. You can feed students any foods you want, as long as they are healthy and delicious.

Write a paragraph explaining your menu.

Be Active Every Day

Write a paragraph explaining why getting exercise every day is important. Illustrate your paragraph.

Journal Entry

Answer Key

page 14 (Food Groups)
Answers will vary; check that answers are reasonably correct.

page 15 (My Plate)
Answers will vary.

page 16 (Think About Fruit) Part I
Answers will vary.

page 17 (Think About Fruit) Part II
Answers will vary.
1. nerves, muscles
2. energy
3. blood cells
4. lungs

page 18 (How Does Fruit Grow?)
Possible answers:
Tree fruits: apples, bananas, cherries, nectarines, oranges, peaches, pears, plums
Bush fruits: blueberries, gooseberries, currants
Bramble fruits: blackberries, raspberries
Vine fruits: cantaloupe, grapes, honeydew, kiwi fruit, watermelon, strawberries
1. Possible answers:
   cucumbers, pumpkin, some squash, tomatoes
2. Answers will vary.

page 19 (Fruit Seeds We Eat)
No answer key necessary.

page 20 (Learn About Mangoes)
Check for appropriate responses.

page 21 (Talk About Fruit)
Answers will vary.

page 22 (Think About Vegetables)
Answers will vary.

page 23 (Culinary or Fruit Vegetables)
1. Cross out asparagus, broccoli, carrot, celery, lettuce, and spinach
2. avocado, bell pepper, cucumber, pumpkin, squash, tomato
3. culinary or fruit vegetables

page 24 (Plant Parts)
roots: beets, carrot, parsnip, potato, radish, rutabaga, sweet potato, turnip, yam
stems: asparagus, bamboo shoots, broccoli, celery, rhubarb
leaves: Brussels sprouts, bok choy, cabbage, collard greens, kale, lettuce, parsley, spinach, watercress
flowers: broccoli, cauliflower
seeds: black beans, corn, kidney beans, lima beans, peas, pinto beans, pumpkin seeds, sunflower seeds
bulbs: garlic, leeks, onion, water chestnuts

page 25 (Where Do Our Vegetables Grow?)
1. Illinois
2. asparagus
3. Answers will vary but should include something about California being an agricultural state providing many different kinds of crops.
4. Answers will vary but might include helping you decide what to purchase and checking what is fresh in season. Shipping would also be a consideration.
5. Answers will vary.

page 26 (Garden to Plate)
No answer key necessary.

page 27 (Farm to Store)
1. Machines plow and prepare the soil. **Production**
2. Farmers plant seeds. **Production**
3. Plants are watered, given nutrients, and weeded. **Production**
4. Vegetables are harvested. **Production**
5. Produce is sorted and cleaned. **Processing**
6. Vegetables are packaged to ship. **Processing**
7. Vegetables travel by truck to the store. **Transportation**
8. Vegetables are sold in stores. **Distribution**

page 28 (Green Is a Great Color)
Show final page.

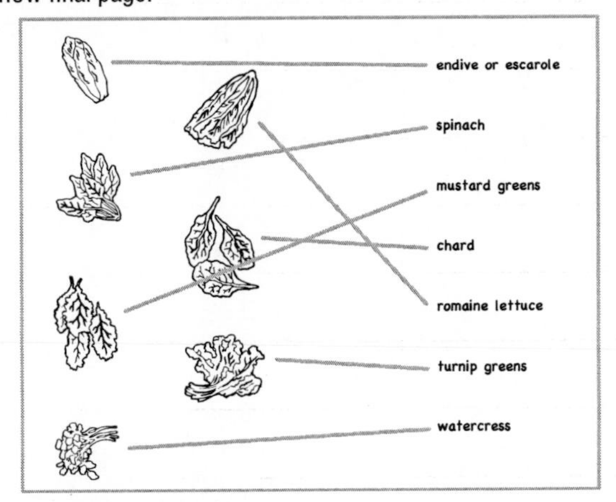

page 29 (New Vegetables)
1. kohlrabi
2. Brussels sprouts
3. artichoke
4. taro
5. romanesco
6. eggplant
7. bok choy
8. watercress
9. rutabaga
10. lentils

Extra question: Answers will vary.

page 30 (Two Kinds of Peppers)
Feel the Heat chart ranking
1—Bell Pepper
2—Banana Pepper
3—Poblano Pepper
4—Anaheim Pepper
5—Jalapeño
6—Serrano Green Chili Pepper
7—Habanero

page 31 (Think About Whole Grains)
1. wheat
2. millet
3. spelt
4. sorghum
5. buckwheat
6. barley
7. amaranth
8. quinoa
9. corn
10. oats
11. bulgur
12. brown rice
13. rye
14. wheat berries

Challenge: Answers will vary.

page 32 (What is a Whole Grain?)

Show final page art.

Diagram should be labeled correctly.

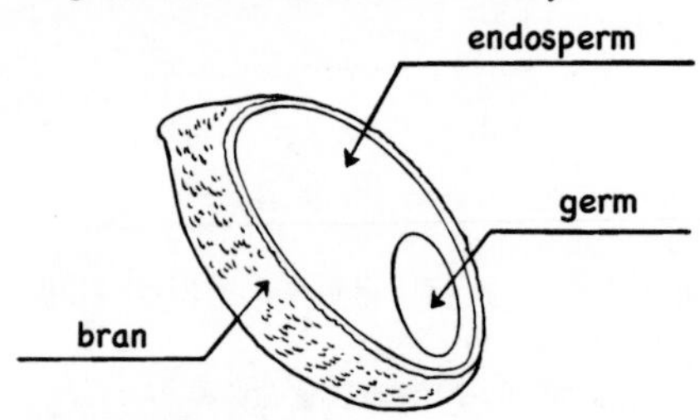

page 33 (Types of Corn)

No answer key necessary.

page 34 (Corn Review Word Search)

Puzzle Solution

A	N	G	E	R	I	A	L	Q	M	H	D
Q	P	R	H	D	S	H	Y	B	W	E	R
H	O	D	O	A	E	Z	A	U	F	Z	L
B	L	R	M	C	H	G	O	N	T	I	Y
U	E	K	I	L	P	A	R	J	F	A	P
X	N	C	N	B	G	O	M	I	D	M	N
J	T	B	Y	N	C	T	P	F	T	E	R
L	A	H	E	T	U	E	X	I	C	S	O
T	D	E	N	T	C	O	R	N	O	G	C
M	G	I	S	A	L	L	I	T	R	O	T
O	L	Z	B	H	N	H	R	D	N	I	E
F	Q	I	T	R	A	C	K	P	M	H	E
S	A	F	O	G	Y	E	N	A	E	N	W
R	N	C	O	R	N	B	R	E	A	D	S
V	E	S	A	C	W	P	D	T	L	Y	C

1. sweet corn
2. dent corn
3. maize
4. popcorn
5. cornmeal
6. mashed hominy, or masa

page 35 (Which Foods have Whole Grains?)

1. underline the following:
   Whole Wheat Bread—Ingredients: <u>whole wheat flour</u>
   Raisin Cereal—Ingredients: <u>whole grain wheat</u>
   Whole Grain Spaghetti—Ingredients: <u>whole durum</u> wheat flour
2. flour tortillas
   The tortillas are made with enriched bleached wheat flour, not whole wheat flour.
3. All of them; answers may vary.

page 36 (Whole Grains Every Day)

Answers will vary.

Here are some tips to help students eat more whole grains:

- Ask grownups to buy whole wheat bread instead of white bread or brown rice instead of white rice.
- Try whole wheat pasta.
- Suggest adding barley to vegetable soup.
- Suggest adding bulgur wheat to stir-fries.
- If students help with making pancakes or waffles, have them help grownups find a whole wheat mix or use whole wheat in the recipe.
- Add unsweetened, whole grain ready-to-eat cereal to salad instead of croutons.
- Snack on ready-to-eat, whole grain cereals such as toasted oat cereal.
- Try 100% whole-grain snack crackers.
- Have popcorn, a whole grain, as a healthy snack after school, with little or no added salt and butter.

page 37 (Think About Dairy Foods)

Answers will vary.

pages 38–39 (How Do We Get Our Milk?)

1. Cows graze on farms. They are fed grains. Their bodies process this food to produce milk.
2. Cows are milked with milking machines.
3. Milk is put in refrigerated tanks immediately to prevent the growth of harmful bacteria.
4. Milk is tested by farmers.
5. Trucks transport milk from farm to factory and workers test the milk again.
6. Milk is pasteurized (heated) to kill harmful bacteria.
7. Milk is homogenized to prevent any remaining fat particles from rising to the top of the milk and forming a cream layer. This step gives milk a more consistent texture and appearance.
8. Milk is put into jugs or containers.
9. Trucks transport the milk containers to stores for purchase.

page 40 (What's the Difference?)

Accept reasonable answers for the Venn diagram:

regular yogurt: not as much protein, more carbohydrates, not as thick

Greek yogurt: strained; whey, lactose, some sugar removed; thicker; more protein; fewer carbohydrates and lower sugar; tastes creamier

both: healthy dairy food, live bacterial cultures, calcium, can be low calorie

page 41 (Eating Dairy Foods)

Possible answers:

1. I can have *milk* in a bowl of *cereal.*
2. I can make a *dip* for vegetables out of *yogurt.*
3. I can put a slice of *cheese* on a *sandwich* for lunch.
4. I can make a *smoothie* out of fruit and *yogurt.*
5. I can stir some *fruit* into *yogurt* for a tasty breakfast or lunch.
6. I can have a *glass* of *milk* at dinner.
7. I can add *cheese* to my *taco.*
8. I can have *cheese* with whole grain *crackers* instead of a sandwich at lunch.
9. Answers will vary.

page 42 (Think About Protein Foods)

Answers will vary.

pages 43–44 (Beef Is a Source of Protein)

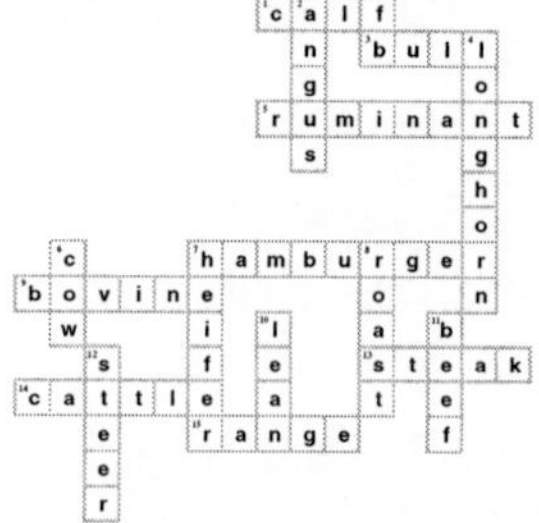

Across

1. A <u>calf</u> is a young male or female cow less than one year of age.
3. A <u>bull</u> is a mature male bovine that can reproduce.
5. A <u>ruminant</u> is an animal that eats plants and converts them into meat or milk that humans can eat.
7. A <u>hamburger</u> is made from ground beef.
9. The term <u>bovine</u> refers to cattle.
13. A <u>steak</u> is a thick slice of beef cut across the muscle grain.
14. Cows, bulls, and steers have horns and are raised for food or for their hides. They are also know as <u>cattle</u>.
15. Cattle graze on an area of open, grassy land called a <u>range</u>.

pages 43–44 (Beef Is a Source of Protein) (*cont.*)

Down

2. Angus is a breed of cattle known for tender beef.
4. The earliest breed of cattle raised for beef in the United States is the Texas longhorn.
6. A mature female that has produced a calf is called a cow.
7. A female cow over one year old that has not had a calf is called a heifer.
8. Roast beef is cooked in a hot oven.
10. Meat that is lean has little or no fat.
11. The meat that comes from the muscle of an adult cow is called beef.
12. A steer is an adult male cow raised as beef for people to eat.

page 45 (Fish—Protein and Good Fat)

1. *shellfish circled:* clams, crab, crayfish, lobster, scallops, shrimp

S	C	A	L	L	O	P	S	D	L
B	W	L	E	C	F	H	[illegible]	Y	O
H	C	O	R	T	R	M	[illegible]	C	[illegible]
[illegible]	O	A	R	I	F	T	[illegible]	[illegible]	S
[illegible]	B	S	M	D	O	S	[illegible]	[illegible]	[illegible]
[illegible]	S	P	G	R	T	T	[illegible]	[illegible]	[illegible]
[illegible]	U	N	A	K	U	I	H	[illegible]	R
[illegible]	C	E	A	B	A	S	S	[illegible]	G
C	E	G	I	R	G	M	B	H	P
S	A	L	M	O	N	Y	R	N	A
N	A	R	L	S	M	A	L	C	S
H	S	I	F	Y	A	R	C	W	B

page 46 (Legumes for Protein and More!)

```
       LENTILS
CHICKPEAS
       GARBANZO BEANS
  PEANUTS
       MUNG BEANS
      PEAS
 BEAN SPROUTS
```

Legume Clues

1. lentils
2. chickpeas
3. garbanzo beans
4. peanuts
5. mung beans
6. peas
7. bean sprouts

page 47 (Nuts About Protein)

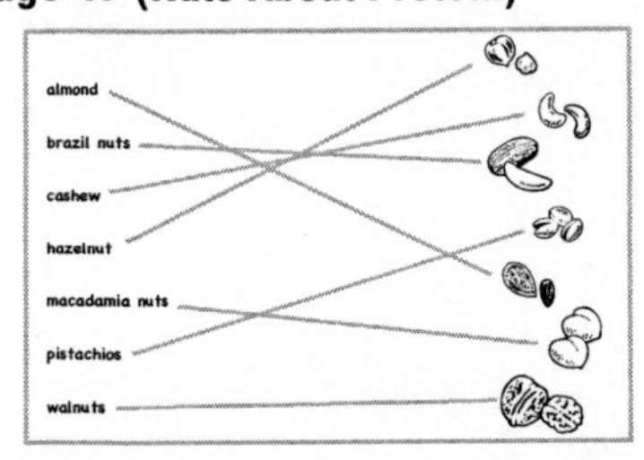

page 48 (Making Healthy Food Choices)

Answers will vary.

page 49 (Vitamins and Minerals Chart)

No answer key necessary.

page 50 (Vitamins)

Possible answers:

1. broccoli, carrots, cheese, milk, spinach
2. broccoli
3. cabbage, orange, strawberries
4. dark-green vegetables, eggs
5. Vitamins A and E.
6. dried beans, eggs, or meat
7. whole grains, eggs, or milk
8. tomatoes, strawberries; cabbage, peas
9. eggs, green, leafy vegetables, whole grains
10. eggs, meat

page 51 (Vitamins and Minerals)

Possible answers:

1. citrus fruits (orange)
2. vitamin K
3. calcium, vitamin K
4. B-vitamins help our bodies use energy from food and keep our blood healthy.
5. Vitamin A helps us maintain healthy hair, skin, and vision.
6. Vitamin C keeps our muscles, teeth, and gums healthy. It protects us from infection and helps us heal.
7. Potassium; potassium helps us maintain healthy muscles, cells, and nerves; helps our body use energy from food.
8. Leafy green vegetables have many vitamins and other nutrients to help us maintain healthy bodies.
9. Vitamin D helps us use calcium from the foods we eat to promote strong bones and teeth.
10. Dried beans and peas provide many different nutrients, such as folic acid, calcium, phosphorus, potassium, and iron. These nutrients help us maintain healthy blood cells and muscles.

page 52 (Calories Equal Energy)

Answers will vary.

page 53 (What Is Junk Food?)

Answers will vary.

page 54 (What Is Fiber?)

1. baked potato
2. baked potato
3. Answers will vary.

page 55 (What Is Cholesterol?)

1. HDL carries cholesterol back to liver, exercise helps the body use HDL, and helps digest food
   LDL carries cholesterol into body, can stick to blood vessels, cause heart disease or stroke, found in saturated and trans fats.
2. Eat low-fat foods and get enough exercise.

Challenge: Answers will vary.

page 56 (Sodium)

Answers will vary. Check for understanding.

page 57 (Sugar)

Answers will vary. Check for understanding.

page 58 (Added Sugar)

Do the math: 6 teaspoons of sugar equals 24 grams of sugar.
Kids should have no more than 24 grams of added sugar per day.

barbecue sauce	3 teaspoons
graham crackers	2 teaspoons
granola bars	8g
peanut butter	less than 1 teaspoon
raisin bran cereal	16g
saltine crackers	0g
spaghetti sauce	2 teaspoons
yogurt	24g

1. Answers will vary.
2. granola bars and spaghetti sauce

page 59 (Why Water?)

1. Students should color 6 glasses.
2. Kids should color 1 ½ glasses.
3. Answers will vary but may include the following:
   helps us digest food
   carries nutrients to parts of our bodies
   keeps eyes moist, helps joints move
   helps us eat the right amount of food.

page 60 (Food Tips for Tip-Top Health)
Answers will vary.

page 61 (How Much Is a Serving?)
No answer key necessary.

page 62 (Plan a Menu)
Answers will vary.

page 63 (So Many Healthy Foods!)

1. corn
2. cheese
3. sunflower seeds
4. kiwi fruit
5. avocado
6. celery

page 64 (Food Safety)

1. Boy is sneezing on food.
   Meat and vegetables are on the same cutting board. Check other answers for reasonableness.
2. Answers will vary.
3. Answers will vary.

page 65 (Healthy Lifestyles)
Answers will vary.

page 66 (Make a "Healthy Me" Mini-Book)
No answer key necessary.

page 67 (Dental Health)

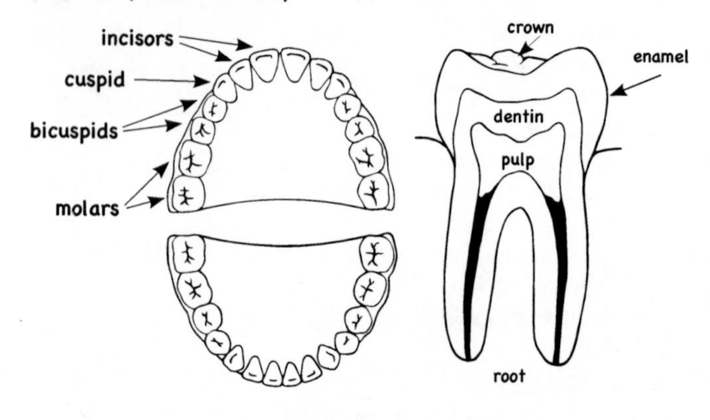

page 68 (Get Enough Sleep)
1–5 Answers will vary.

page 69 (Physical Safety)
Accept reasonable answers.

Getting Around Town

1. crosswalk
2. traffic; cars
3. cars
4. bushes or trees; trash cans, walls, or parked vehicles.
5. space
6. helmet
7. rules

School Bus Safety

1. quietly
2. clear
3. safety
4. away
5. signal
6. crossing

Stranger Danger

1. know
2. help; protect
3. no, Tell
4. rules
5. Answers will vary.

page 70 (Physical Fitness)

1. False
2. True
3. True
4. False
5. True
6. False
7. True
8. False
9. False
10. True

page 71 (Heart Rate)
Answers will vary.

page 72 (Beanbags and Relays)
No answer key necessary.

page 73 (Active Days)
Check sentences for appropriate use of action words.

page 74 (Machine Movements)

1. Accept reasonable choices. Possible answers.

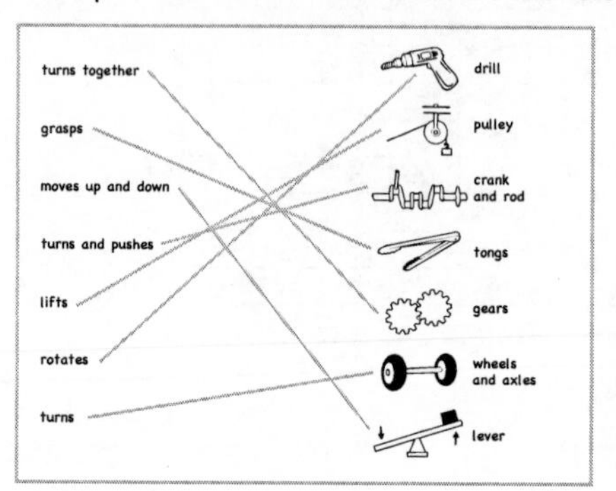

2. Answers will vary.

page 75 (Sports Field Day)
Check for reasonable answers.
Basketball: passing, throwing (shooting toward a target), catching, dribbling, defending, stopping, pivoting
Soccer: dribbling, passing, trapping (ball control), defending, kicking, throwing, shooting (toward a target), goalkeeping
Baseball: gripping, throwing, pitching, fielding, catching, batting, bunting, running
Football: passing, catching, handing off the ball, blocking, kicking
Swimming: paddling, kicking, pushing, pulling, arm circles
Hockey: gripping, carrying, dribbling, passing, fielding, tackling, dodging, goalkeeping
Volleyball: serving, throwing, passing, jumping
Track and Field: running, jumping, hurdling

page 76 (Summer Fun)
Answers will vary; check for reasonable answers.

page 77 (Fitness Challenge)
Answers will vary.

page 78 (The World Around You)
Answers will vary.

page 79 (Healthy Habits Game)
No answer key necessary.

page 80 (Relay Activities)
No answer key necessary.

page 81 (Outdoor Activities)
No answer key necessary.